# ARMY REGULATIONS, INDIA

## Volume VII

---

# DRESS.

# Agents for the Sale of Books published by the Superintendent of Government Printing, India, Calcutta

### IN THE UNITED KINGDOM

Messrs CONSTABLE & Co, 10 Orange Street Leicester Square, London, W C
Messrs KEGAN PAUL TRENCH TRÜBNER & Co., 68 74 Carter Lane E C
Mr. BERNARD QUARITCH, 11 Grafton Street, New Bond Street London W
Messrs P. S KING & SON 2 and 4 Great Smith Street Westminster, London, S W
Messrs H. S. KING & Co 65 Cornhill and 9, Pall Mall London.
Messrs. GRINDLAY & Co 54 Parliament Street London, S W
Mr. T. FISHER UNWIN 1, Adelphi Terrace London, W C
Messrs W. THACKER & Co, 2 Creed Lane London E.C
Messrs. LUZAC & Co 46 Great Russell Street, London, W C
Mr. B H BLACKWELL 50 and 51 Broad Street Oxford.
Messrs DEIGHTON BELL & Co Cambridge
Messrs OLIVER AND BOYD Tweeddale Court Edinburgh.
Messrs. E PONSONBY LD 116 Grafton Street Dublin

### ON THE CONTINENT

Mr OTTO HARRASSOWITZ Leipzig
Mr CARL W HIERSEMANN Leipzig
Messrs R FRIEDLANDER & SOHN Berlin W N Carlestrasse, 11
Mr. ERNEST LEROUX 28 Rue Bonaparte Paris France
Mr MARTINUS NIJHOFF The Hague, Holland

### IN INDIA AND CEYLON

Messrs. THACKER SPINK & Co Calcutta and Simla
Messrs NEWMAN & Co, Calcutta.
Messrs R CAMBRAY & Co Calcutta
Messrs S K. LAHIRI & Co Calcutta
Messrs B BANERJEE & Co., Calcutta
THE CALCUTTA SCHOOL BOOK AND USEFUL LITERATURE SOCIETY, 309 Bowbazar Street Calcutta
Messrs BUTTERWORTH & Co (India) Ld, Calcutta

### IN INDIA AND CEYLON—contd

THE WELDON LIBRARY, 18 5, Chowringhee Calcutta
Messrs HIGGINBOTHAM & Co, Madras
Messrs V KALYANARAMA IYER & Co Madras.
Messrs G A NATESAN & Co. Madras
Messrs S MURTHY & Co Madras
Messrs THOMPSON & Co., Madras
Messrs TEMPLE & Co, Madras.
Messrs COMBRIDGE & Co Madras.
Messrs P R RAMA IYER & Co., Madras
Messrs THACKER & Co LD Bombay.
Messrs A J COMBRIDGE & Co Bombay
Messrs. D B TARAPOREVALA SONS & Co Bombay
Mrs RADHABAI ATMARAM SAGOON Bombay
Mr SUNDER PANDURANG Bombay
Messrs GOPAL NARAYAN & Co Bombay
Messrs RAM CHANDRA GOVIND & SON, Kalbadevi, Bombay.
Mr. N B. MATHI R, Superintendent, Nazir Kanun Hind Press, Allahabad
RAI SAHIB M GULAB SINGH & SONS Mufid i Am Press Lahore and Calcutta.
SUPERINTENDENT AMERICAN BAPTIST MISSION PRESS Rangoon
Messrs. A CHAND & Co., Punjab
Babu S. C TALUKDAR Proprietor, Students & Co Cooch Behar.
Messrs A M & J FERGUSON Colombo Ceylon
Manager, Educational Book Depôts Nagpur and Jubbulpur *
Manager of the Imperial Book Depôt, 63 Chandney Chauk Street, Delhi *
Manager East Coast News Vizagapatam *
Manager The Agra Medical Hall and Co operative Association, Limited (Successors to A JOHN & Co, Agra) *
Superintendent Basel Mission Book and Tract Depository Mangalore *
Messrs P. VARADACHARY & Co MADRAS *
Mr. H LIDDELL, Printer, etc, 7 South Road Allahabad *
Messrs D C ANAND & SONS Peshawar

N B.—[Those marked with an asterisk (*) are agents for sale of Legislative Department publications only ]

# ARMY REGULATIONS, INDIA,
## VOLUME VII

# DRESS

Government of India
Army Department, 1913

CALCUTTA
SUPERINTENDENT GOVERNMENT PRINTING INDIA
1913

First published in 1913 by
The Government of India Army Department


ISBN 1 871167 19 1

Printed & bound by Antony Rowe Ltd, Eastbourne

# PREFACE

THIS volume contains the orders of the Government of India on the Dress of the Army in India and is to be read in conjunction with Dress Regula tions for the Army (made applicable to the British Services on the Indian establishment by India Army Order 448 of 1912), and the King's Regulations

General or other Officers Commanding will be held responsible that no deviations from the authorized patterns in the uniform of officers, warrant officers and soldiers, nor mixed orders of dress, are permitted in their commands

*(This book is corrected up to 1st January 1913 )*

**W R BIRDWOOD**, *Major General,*
*Secretary to the Government of India, Army Department*

# TABLE OF CONTENTS

## PART I

## PART II

## PART III

## PART IV

## PART V

## PART VI

## PART VII

## PART VIII

## PART IX

# PART X

## APPENDICES

# ARMY REGULATIONS, INDIA

## VOLUME VII — DRESS

## 1912

---

## PART I

### GENERAL INSTRUCTIONS AND ORDERS OF DRESS

1  Commanding Officers are forbidden to introduce or to sanction any deviation from the sealed patterns of dress, clothing, equipment and badges    They will be responsible for replacing or restoring to the approved pattern any articles worn in their units which may be found not to be in conformity therewith

2  They will however permit individual officers to continue to wear articles of dress already in their use which become obsolete by change of pattern in regulations    No permission to continue the wear of obsolete articles will extend beyond five years from the change of regulations, such articles may not be renewed, but must be replaced by the latest patterns

3  When obtaining uniform and equipment, officers should make sure, by personal comparison, if possible, that articles are being supplied according to sealed pattern

Officers are permitted to purchase such articles of clothing, necessaries materials suitable for their uniforms and equipment as may be available from the Army Clothing and Ordnance Factories or regimental stores

4  No unauthorized ornament or emblem is to be worn when in uniform, but special emblems may be carried on the headdress on anniversaries, provided authority has been obtained

5  A sprig of shamrock may be worn by Irishmen in their headdress on St Patrick's day

6  Officers on leave are to be in possession of uniform for use if detailed for duty    Officers while in foreign countries are not to wear uniform without having obtained the permission of His Majesty's representative, which will only be granted when they are employed on duty, or attending court, or at State ceremonies to which they have been invited    Permission to wear uniform at foreign manœuvres can only be obtained from the War Office.

7  Regulation uniform must not be worn at fancy dress balls but there is no objection to military uniform of obsolete pattern being worn on such occasions

8  Uniform will be worn while on duty

9  Officers attending as spectators on occasions when troops parade under arms will wear the same order of dress as the troops

### GENERAL INSTRUCTIONS

10  **Aiguillette** —The aiguillette is the distinguishing mark of officers serving on the Staff of the army and in Personal Appointments    See para 83

For description and method of wearing it, see para 76

The aiguillette for Field Marshals Personal Appointments to the King and Royal Family is included in the description of their respective uniforms in Dress Regulations for the Army    That for Personal Appointments to the Viceroy and Governor General of India in the description of their uniform—paras 61 to 71

11  **Badges of Rank** —The rank of officers is shown by badges as under : —

*Field Marshal* —Crossed batons on a wreath of laurel, with a crown above
*General* —Crossed sword and baton, with crown and star above
*Lieutenant General* —Crossed sword and baton, with crown above
*Major General* —Crossed sword and baton with star above
*Brigadier General* —Crossed sword and baton
*Colonel* —Crown and two stars below
*Lieutenant Colonel* —Crown and one star below
*Major* —Crown

*Captain* —Three stars

*Lieutenant* —Two stars

*Second-Lieutenant* — One star

Badges of rank, except when otherwise ordered, will be worn on all shoulder cords and shoulder straps  They will be in silver embroidery on gold shoulder cords and gold laced shoulder straps, in gilt or gilding metal on plain cloth shoulder straps and in gold embroidery on the frock coat  Regiments dressed in green, bronze; and those in drab, silver, except where otherwise stated in the description of uniforms of the several units

The crowns when laid on shoulder cords or shoulder straps are 1 inch broad and 1 inch in height; the stars are 1 inch between opposite points

The batons forming part of the Field Marshal's badges will be in embroidery and crimson velvet  General Officer's badges are worn in pairs, point of the sword to the front and edge of blade outwards  or towards the arm  The sword is 2 inches long and the baton $\frac{1}{2}$ inch shorter

Officers having brevet, local, temporary, or honorary rank wear the badges of that rank

The rank of Indian officers is shown by metal badges worn on  the shoulder straps as under :—

*Risaldar Ma or and Subadar Major* —Crown

*Risaldar, Ressaidar, Subadar and Senior Sub Assistant Surgeon, 1st Class* — Two stars

*Jemadar and Senior Sub Assistant Surgeon, 2nd Class* —One star

12  **Badges** —No badges are allowed to be worn, except those authorized by these and the Dress Regulations for the Army  Civil insignia, mayoral chains and badges are not to be worn with military uniform

Collar badges will be fixed with the centre of the badge 2 inches from the opening of the collar of the tunic or frock coat

13  **Badges, Special.**—Regimental badges, devices and other distinctions granted under special authority are to be strictly preserved  Badges are to be metal unless otherwise ordered  For detailed descriptions see Appx I  Badges may be worn on the collar of mess dress

Officers of regiments of the Indian Army wearing silvered appointments wear German silver titles on the shoulder cords or straps

14. **Belts, Sword** —As described for the respective services

They will be worn as follows :—

(1) The web sword belt, described in Appendix II (*b*), will be worn under the tunic, and over the fiock coat and kurta (under the sash or girdle) by all officers for whom it is the prescribed full dress belt  Infantry officers carrying colours wear the web sword belt over the tunic and under the sash

(2) Other full dress sword belts will be worn over the tunic, frock coat and kurta

The web belt will be worn under patrol jackets, serge and white frocks by officers of all branches of the service  Slings will be fitted with studs and holes so that they can be removed from the belt  At balls and entertainments when the sword is allowed to be taken off, officers who wear the belt over the tunic will continue to wear sword belt and slings  Other officers will remove them

15  **Belts, " Sam Browne "**—The universal pattern, " Sam Browne " in brown (or black) leather, with one or two braces, revolver case, ammunition pouch, frog and brown (or black) leather scabbard is worn with service dress— Appendix II (*a*)

In regiments of the Indian Army in which the men wear belts similar to the " Sam Browne " the officers may wear the same pattern  if desired regimentally

16  **Boots** —(*For occasions on which worn see Orders of Dress* )

Butcher —The height of the boot will vary according to the length of the leg  It should reach to about 4 inches from the top of the knee  The leg should be jacked sufficiently to prevent it sinking  A spur rest is fixed  2 inches above the edge of the heel to keep the spur horizontal

Wellington —Plain black and patent leather

Ankle —Brown or black, according to the colour of the uniform, with plain toe caps   Worn with putties or leggings, at the option of regiments, but all officers of a unit must be dressed alike

17  **Breeches, Service Dress** —Bedford cord and khaki drill for mounted officers will be laced at the knee   Colour of Bedford cord for mounted officers of the British Service to be that in use in England.

Khaki Jodhpur breeches with ankle boots without spurs may be worn by officers of British and Indian Cavalry regiments and Royal Horse and Field Artillery units at musketry, stables and in camp

18  **Cap, Field** —Regimental pattern, may be worn in camp, on service, and at manœuvres   Its upkeep is optional

19  **Cap, Forage, Universal Pattern—**

Cloth, with three cloth welts, $4\frac{1}{4}$ inches total depth, diameter across the top $10\frac{3}{8}$ inches for a cap fitting $21\frac{3}{4}$ inches in circumference, the top to be $\frac{1}{8}$ inch larger or smaller in diameter for every $\frac{1}{4}$ inch the cap may vary in size of head above or below the before mentioned standard, e g , a cap $22\frac{1}{2}$ inches in circum ference, diameter across the top $10\frac{5}{8}$ inches ; cap 21 inches in circumference, diameter 10 inches   The sides to be made in four pieces, and to be $2\frac{1}{2}$ inches deep between the welts, a cloth band $1\frac{1}{2}$ inches wide placed between the two lower welts

The cap set up on a band of stiff leather, or other material, $1\frac{1}{4}$ inches deep, but not stiffened up in front

Chin strap of black patent leather $\frac{3}{8}$ inch wide, buttoned on to two  $\frac{1}{2}$ inch gilt buttons placed immediately behind the corners of the peak

The peak to droop at an angle of 45 degrees, and to be 2 inches deep in the middle when worn with embroidery, and $1\frac{1}{4}$ inches when plain

Peaks will be embroidered as follows : —

*Field Marshals and General Officers* —Two rows of oakleaf embroidery

*Field Officers on the Staff of the Army* —One row of oakleaf embroidery on lower edge

*Other Field Officers* —Plain gold embroidery $\frac{3}{4}$ inch wide on lower edge

*Field Officers of Rifle Regiments and Indian Infantry dressed in green or drab.*—Black or drab oakleaf embroidery on lower edge

*Other Officers* —Plain peak

*Indian Cavalry* —Cap, colour of tunic : band and welts, colour of facings, except 1st Lancers, cap blue, band yellow : 12th and 16th Cavalry, band and welts, yellow

*Indian Infantry* —Regiments dressed in scarlet—cap, blue cloth ; band, black, oakleaf braid, scarlet welt on crown

Regiments dressed in green—cap, rifle green cloth ; band, black mohair braid (2nd Gurkha Rifles, red and black diceboard) black welts

Regiments dressed in drab—cap, drab cloth ; band drab mohair braid ; welt on crown, colour of facings

*I M S* —Cap, blue cloth ; band, black velvet

*S and T Corps, including Departmental Officers with honorary rank* —Cap, blue cloth ; band, blue ; welts, white

*Departmental Officers with honorary rank other than S and T Corps —* Universal pattern  cap without welts but with  distinctive band 2 inches wide all round   This band will be detachable

The bands are of the following descriptions : —

*Army Clothing Department* —Light blue cloth with $\frac{1}{8}$ inch dark blue welt down the centre

*Army Remount Department.*—Yellow cloth, $\frac{1}{8}$ inch light blue down the centre

*I S. M D* —Blue cloth with black braid down the centre

*Military Farms Department* —Grass green, $\frac{1}{8}$ inch light scarlet down the centre

*Military Works Department, including Barrack, Public Works, Telegraph, and Sappers and Miners* —Blue cloth with $\frac{1}{8}$ inch light scarlet down the centre

*Miscellaneous List, Military Accounts and Garrison and Depôt Staff* —Blue cloth with scarlet piping on both edges

*Ordnance Department* —Scarlet cloth, $\frac{1}{8}$ inch light blue down the centre

*Superintendents, Detention Barracks and Military Prisons*—Scarlet cloth
¼ inch edging of black mohair braid all round

Forage caps will be placed evenly on the head.

20  **Covers to Forage Caps**—In India a khaki cover will be worn with khaki uniform ; a white cover at all other times   It should cover the top and sides of the cap only, the distinctive band should not be covered   Elsewhere the local orders will be followed

21  **Collars**—The collars of tunics, frock coats, and jackets will, unless other wise stated, be cut square at the top in front, and fastened with two hooks and eyes ; a silk tab sewn on inside   The height is not to exceed 2 inches

White linen collars are worn with the serge frock and mess dress   With frock coat, white frock and khaki jacket they are optional, but all officers of a unit must be dressed alike   The collar is not to show more than ½ inch above the stand up collar of the uniform

A white linen collar will not be worn in mess dress when the waistcoat is closed up to the neck

For description of collars worn with open fronted service dress jacket see para. 31

22  **Depth of Skirts**—The skirts of tunics for officers 5 feet 9 inches in height will be :—

For all officers except those of Cavalry and Rifle regiments, 10 inches—For officers of Cavalry and Rifle regiments, 9 inches   The skirts of frock-coats will reach to the knees

Indian Infantry regiments dressed in green and drab conform to the orders for British Rifle regiments

23  **Foot-straps.**—Black leather

24  **Frock Coat, Universal**—Blue cloth, double breasted, with stand up collar ; plain sleeves with two small buttons and button holes at the bottom ; two rows of large regimental buttons down the front, six in each row at equal distances, the distance between the rows 8 inches at the top and 4½ inches at the bottom, *these measurements are not to be exceeded ;* flaps behind 10 inches deep, one button on each flap and one on each side of the waist ; the skirt to reach to the knees and to be lined ; shoulder straps of cloth the same material as the garment attached by an under piece passed through a loop on the lower part of the shoulder, fastened at the top by a small button which passes through both under piece and shoulder strap ; the top of the strap is triangular   Collar badges, according to unit Badges of rank in gold embroidery, on shoulder straps

In the Indian Army this garment is only worn by General Officers, for whom it is obligatory, and Staff Officers, for whom it is optional

25  **Frock, Serge, Universal**—Blue angola tartan, or serge   In regiments dressed in green and drab the frock will be the colour of the uniform

*(The specification of the latest pattern will be issued as an amendment as soon as received from the War Office   In the meantime existing patterns may be worn as provided for in paragraph 2 )*

26  **Gloves**—Full dress and with frock coat and serge frock when worn in Undress Order No. 5—White doe or buckskin   Indian Infantry regiments dressed in green black leather ; in drab, brown or drab leather

In all other Orders of Dress—Brown, drab or black leather according to the colour of the uniform

All officers of a unit must wear the same pattern.

At Levées and Balls   All officers will wear white kid gloves, except those of regiments, which wear black gloves at levées

Gloves will not be worn in hot weather, with white uniform, or Service Dress.

27  **Gorget Patches** (*see also paras 78 and 83*)—Worn with Service Dress   With the khaki drill jacket they will be detachable

In the services below, a gorget patch 2¾ inches long and 1¼ inch wide, pointed at the outer end, is worn on each side of the collar of the Service Dress jacket

#### (a) By all officers

*Army Clothing Department* —Light blue cloth, with a double row of dark blue braid down the centre.

*Army Ordnance Department* —Blue cloth with line of scarlet Russia braid, a gorget departmental button near the point

*Army Veterinary Service* —Maroon cloth, a gorget corps button near the point   Colonels have a line of scarlet Russia braid along the centre

*Inspector of Army Schools* —Blue cloth with light blue line, a gorget departmental button near the point

*General Officer* —Scarlet cloth, a line of gold Russia braid along the centre, with a gold net button near the point

*Medical Services—Surgeon General* —Black velvet a line of gold Russia braid along the centre, with a gold net button near the point   *Colonel* —Black velvet, a line of scarlet Russia braid along the centre, gorget button near the point   *Other Officers* —Blue (I M S and I S M D  Black) cloth with line of black Russia tracing, a gorget corps button  near the point

*Military Accounts Department* —Blue cloth with a single row  of scarlet braid carried all round

*Ordnance Department in India* —Blue cloth with two distinctive rows of scarlet braid, a gorget departmental button near the point

*S and T Corps* — Blue cloth, with a line of white braid, gorget corps buttons near the point

*Substantive Colonel and Staff Officer* —Scarlet cloth with line of scarlet silk Russia braid, instead of gold, and gorget button near the point

#### (b) By Departmental Officers with Honorary Rank

*Army Remount Department* —Yellow cloth, with a double row of dark blue braid down the centre

*Military Farms Department* —Grass green, with a double row of scarlet braid down the centre

*Military Works Department, including Barracks, Public Works, Telegraph and Sappers and Miners* —Blue cloth, with a double row of scarlet braid down the centre

*Miscellaneous List* —Blue cloth with a single row of scarlet braid carried all round

28  **Great Coat, Universal** —Cloth, drab mixture, milled and water proofed; double breasted, to reach within a foot of the ground; stand and fall collar 5 inches deep (2 inch stand and 3 inch fall), fastening with two hooks and eyes; cloth tab and buttons; a 2¼ inch inverted expanding pleat down the centre of the back, from the collar to the waist terminating under the back strap; ordinary sleeves, loose turn back cuffs of single material, 6 inches deep; two large cross pockets with slightly curved flaps at the waist in front; vertical slit for sword jetted in left side 1½ inches above the pocket; a pocket in the left breast placed vertically between the second and third buttons; two rows of buttons down the front, four in each row, about 6½ inches apart  the rows 8 inches apart at the top and  4 inches at the bottom; two buttons to back slit with holes in a fly; a 2 inch cloth back strap sewn in side seams fastened with three holes and buttons; skirt to fasten with two tabs and buttons inside, and to run squarely all round ; coat lined on shoulder and sleeve only ; shoulder straps of same material as the garment, sewn  on to the shoulder at base and fastened at the top by a small button ; the top of the strap is triangular   Buttons and badges of rank in gilt metal   The coat is cut below the waist with spring to form 8 inch lap, or  4 inches on from the centre line   The slit at the back should be of suitable length for riding

29  **Helmet, Universal, Foreign Service** —Helmets in drill covers of the following description are worn by all officers :—

#### White

" Wolseley " pattern, cork, made with six seams ; bound with buff leather ;

projecting brim all round, 3 inches in front, 4 inches at back, 2 inches at sides; ventilated at top with zinc button covered with khaki or white drill; side hooks  At top of helmet, a collet riveted on to a collar ⅜ inch wide to receive the button  Brown or black leather chin strap ⅜ inch wide  The khaki helmet with a white cover and white pagri may be substituted for the white helmet

The badge is worn in the centre of the pagri or on the front of the helmet, when it is of a size which cannot be conveniently attached to the pagri  For description of Badges see Appx I  Unless a special badge for the helmet is described that for the forage cap is worn on the pagri

The chin chain, links ⅜ inch wide, is lined with white or drab leather  Regiments dressed in green have a chain on morocco leather of the colour of the regimental facings, lined with black velvet

Hackles may be worn on the full dress headdress by regiments for which they are authorised

Lines when worn are fastened to a small ring at the back of the helmet underneath the brim

Ornaments, unless otherwise stated, will be in gilt or gilding metal ; bronze in regiments dressed in green or drab

Cavalry —A spike of bright metal, on a dead base,—acanthus leaf pattern

Dimensions : —

Height of spike from base, 3⅜ inches

Total height of spike and base, 4⅛ inches

Diameter of spike at point of contact with leaf base, 1 inch

Diameter of base, 3¼ inches

The base has eight principal points, with an interval of about 1¼ inches between each point

In the Royal Horse and Field Artillery, Ordnance Department in India, Royal Army Medical Corps, Indian Medical Service, Army Veterinary Corps, a ball in a leaf on the cup, pattern of base as for Cavalry  The height of the ball and cup is 1¾ inches  In the Royal Garrison Artillery the ball in leaf cup is mounted on the dome base as for Infantry

Royal Engineers, Infantry, and Army Ordnance Department —Spike of metal, mounted on a dome base

Dimensions :—

Height of spike from place of insertion in dome, 2¾ inches

Total height of spike and dome, 3¼ inches

Diameter of spike at point of contact with dome, 1 inch

Diameter of dome, 1⅜ inches

Circumference of dome at point of contact with helmet, 5⅞ inches

White pagris are worn with white helmets, Regimental pattern pagris may be worn when authorised

Plumes, or spikes, and chains are worn on the white helmet by all officers ; but only on ceremonial occasions when not on parade with their men by officers of British regiments in which the men do not wear such ornaments  Plumes are not worn by General and Staff Officers and officers holding Personal Appointments when in Review Order— Staff in blue

Plumes : General and Staff Officers—White swan feathers, drooping outwards, with red feathers under, reaching to the end of the white ones  Military Secretaries and Aides de Camp wear the red feathers outside the white  Officers of Royal Engineers and Departmental Officers who wear the cocked hat at home—Plumes of the description and colour laid down for their respective services

Plumes are attached to the helmet by means of a screw passing through a socket 1½ inches high, leaf pattern, and fastened by a nut

The feathers of plumes will be, for general officers, 10 inches ; colonels, 8 inches ; and officers under the rank of colonel, 6 inches in length

*Khaki.*

The same pattern as the white helmet, with a plain khaki pagri  Plumes, spikes, chains and metal badges are not worn

British Officers serving with Indian units are permitted to wear a lungi in the place of a helmet with khaki dress, except Infantr ᵣ in Full dress   All Officers of a unit must be dressed alike

30 **Hot Weather Uniform, White** —(*Optional for   Indian Army, except Staff and Departments, see also para. 55* )

*Frock* —White drill, full in the chest  patch pockets with pointed flaps and small button on each side of breast outside   and with a one inch box pleat down the centre, left open so as to admit of expansion ; the pockets to be slightly round ed off at bottom   6½ inches deep and 6¼ inches broad at the top (outside measure ments with centre pleat closed) ;  the edge of the pocket flaps to be in line one inch below the second button   Shoulder straps to be of the same material as the garment, fastened at the top with a small regulation button, and bearing distinc tive metal letters  or  numerals  indicating  the  corps,  regiment or department. Badges of rank in metal   Stand up collar rounded off in front with one hook   Five small buttons of regulation pattern down the front   One inside pocket Cuffs pointed 5 inches high at the point and 2½ inches behind   The frock to be of sufficient length just to clear the saddle when mounted

*Highland and Scottish Regiments.*—As above except cuffs to be gauntlet shape 5 inches deep at the back seam and 3½ inches at the front seam   Skirt rounded off in front to clear the top of the sporran

*Trousers* —White drill   Black  leather  foot straps  obligatory for  mounted officers

*Mess Dress*

*Kamarbands*—Will be  of silk in the following colours :—

| | |
|---|---|
| Staff                                          . | Red. |
| Indian Cavalry  .        . | Regimental Pattern |
| Indian Infantry dressed in green | Green |
| Indian Infantry dressed in drab | Colour of facings |
| S and T Corps | Blue |
| Military Accounts Department | Blue |
| All  other  Indian  Regiments,  Corps or Departments         . | Red |

For British Service see Dress Regulations for the Army.

*Mess Jacket* —White drill without braid or buttons ; roll collar, shoulder straps of the same material with a small button at top ; one inside breast pocket Sleeves cut plain with pointed cuffs, 5 inches high at point, and 2½ inches behind Badges of rank, metal.   The jacket may also be made with a stand up collar to fasten at the neck with a loop of white cord, but all officers of a unit must have the same pattern

*Trousers* —White drill with black leather foot straps

31 **Jacket, Service Dress.**—Khaki drill or drab serge the latter of the colour in use in England ; single breasted cut as a lounge coat to the waist with a step collar opening 3 inches below the shirt collar  stud or  closed at the neck ; very loose at the chest and shoulders, but fitted at the waist ; a 2½ inches expand ing pleat down the centre of the back, sewn down below the waistband, and a waist seam and band 2¼ inches wide ; military skirt to bottom edge, length of skirt to be 10 inches for an  officer 5 feet 9 inches in height, with proportionate variation for any difference in  height, a hook on each side of the waist ; if the jacket be closed at the neck, it is cut low in the front of the neck with a turn down collar to fasten with one hook and  eye ; tab underneath  with two button holes to button across the opening ; a  2¾ inches fall in front and 2 inches at the back ; collar edge to run V shape showing  top button between.  Two cross patch breast pockets above, 6½ inches wide and 7½ inches deep to the top of the flap ; a 2¼ inches box pleat in the centre ; two expanding  pockets below the waist (pleats at the side), 9¼ inches wide at the top, 10½ inches at the bottom, 8 inches deep to the top of the pocket, fastened at the top with a small button ; flap with button-hole to cover pockets, 3½ inches  deep, 10¾ inches  wide, sewn into bottom edge of waistband   The top of pockets  should  be sewn down at the corners in such a manner that on service the pockets can be expanded  at the top also   Out side ticket pocket in top of the waistband on the right side, inside watch pocket, with a tab  above for chain or strap   Four medium buttons for the open fronted jacket and five for the jacket closed  at the neck  regimental pattern, down the

front the bottom one on lower edge of waistband  Shoulder straps of the same material as the garment, top of the strap triangular, the sides being about 1½ inches long, the button 1 inch from the centre point  The cuffs pointed 5½ inches deep at the point, 2½ inches deep at the back

The jacket will be fitted loosely to admit of warm clothing being worn underneath when necessary

The open fronted jacket will be worn by all General Officers, and officers on the staff of the Army  It may also be worn by all other officers  But all the officers of any unit, corps or department are to wear the same pattern  The open fronted pattern once adopted is not to be changed without the sanction of His Excellency the Commander in Chief

The drab serge service dress jacket described in Dress Regulations for the Army may be worn by officers of the British service but not on parade with their men

The above three patterns of service dress jackets are the only ones permitted to be worn

With the open fronted jacket, a white double collar and a black silk necktie, tied in a sailor knot, will be worn  No gold or other pins are to be placed in the necktie or collar  On field service and manœuvres a turn down khaki collar and a khaki necktie may be worn

British and Indian Officers of Indian Cavalry, Indian Mountain Artillery and Indian Infantry may wear at their option a khaki kurta or blouse on parade with their men of a similar pattern to that worn by the rank and file  All officers of a unit must be dressed alike

32 **Leggings** —With service dress —Plain brown leather  All officers of a unit to wear the same pattern

33 **Mourning Band.**—Crape 3¼ inches wide, worn on the left sleeve, midway between the elbow and the shoulder  Mourning will not be worn at levées or at Court, except when the Court is in mourning

34 **Pea Jacket Khaki** —For General Officers, Substantive Colonels, Staff Officers and all other officers  Khaki tartan, double breasted, cut loose and long enough to cover the service dress jacket; 10 inch slit at back; turn down collar 2 inches deep with lapel and step; four leather buttons on each side, three to button and one under turn  One outside welted breast pocket on left side; two bottom pockets with flap; one watch pocket with flap inside left breast; one inside breast pocket on right side  Two small leather buttons and button holes, 3½-inch slit to cuffs; one row of stitching round cuffs four inches from the end of sleeve  Shoulder straps of the same material as the garment, fastened with a small leather button  Badges of rank in metal  The collar is provided with a tab underneath to button across the opening when required  The provision of this garment is optional, but all officers of a unit must be dressed alike

35 **Putties** —Of the same colour as the men s.

36 **Saddlery** —Universal pattern as in Appendix VI  For colours of brow bands and rosettes for departments and infantry units of the Indian Army, see descriptions of their respective uniforms  Head rope, except as otherwise stated, white cotton

37 **Sashes** —Waist sashes are worn by all officers for whom they are regulation ; tassels hanging from the left side and immediately in rear of the front sling of the sword belt  The tassels should reach 4 inches below the skirt of the tunic  Waist sashes should be 2¾ inches wide and without pleats  Sashes will not be worn in khaki or white uniform except by officers of Highland Regiments when in Review Order, white

38 **Shoulder Chains** —Worn on the kurta and in service dress when worn by the men  They are not to be worn on tunics, frock coats or serge frocks

39 **Shoulder Cords or Shoulder Straps**—Are worn on tunics, jackets, frock coats, serge frocks and great coats

40 **Spurs, Steel.**—With butcher and ankle boots, jack spurs, straps, buckles, and chains  With Wellington boots, box spurs with plain rowels  Spurs will be worn in full dress and service dress by all officers whose duties require them to be mounted  At levées, on ceremonial occasions dismounted, in undress, and in mess dress, spurs will be worn by general officers, staff officers, officers of mounted corps and departments, by field officers, double company com

manders and adjutants of Indian infantry and by field officers of all other services, corps, and departments  They will not be worn on board ship, when travelling, or by officers inspecting armaments or magazines

Double company officers of Indian Infantry will not wear spurs when dis mounted

**41 Swords and Scabbards** —The pattern laid down for the arm of the ser vice  Swords will be carried on parades and duties unless otherwise directed They will not be worn on boardship, at mess, or at stables

Swords will be carried on the saddle by mounted officers in mounted orders of dress, which may include Review Order

The scabbards of officers of dismounted units in Review Order are to be hooked up by those who wear the waist belt over the tunic and carried in the left hand by other officers

**42 Sword Knots** —Worn loose by mounted services in all orders of dress Dismounted services wear the sword knot neatly coiled round the guard of the sword except with the " Sam Browne " belt when it is worn loose

**43. Ties** —Black ties are worn with the open throated serge frock and service dress jacket ; also in mess dress, except by officers of the Oxfordshire and Bucking hamshire Light Infantry who wear white ties  Khaki ties are worn in service dress with khaki shirts  See para 31

**44 Trousers and Pantaloons.** –For mounted officers trousers or overalls should be cut straight, and from 1½ to 2 inches longer than ordinary trousers They should be strapped firmly down to the boot and fit closely above the spurs In mess dress, overalls are worn by all officers except Foot Guards

Pantaloons should be cut loose in the thigh and tight at the knee  Ample length from the hip to the knee is essential so that the wearer can have the ne cessary freedom in mounting and dismounting  They should have buckskin strapping at the knee, and, if made for hard wear, seat strapping also

Pantaloons should be furnished with a waist strap and buckle and with cross pockets

**45 Waterproof** —Atholl grey for General Officers, Colonels and officers who wear the Atholl grey great coat  Drab mixture for all other officers.  Single breasted " Inverness," whole back with centre slit, hole and button ; five bone buttons down the front ; cape, four bone buttons ; cross pockets patched on inside with flaps ; sword slit at left side ; three inch turn down collar with detach able tab ; two long body straps, crossing over chest and fastening with hole and button at waist behind ; two short straps with holes and buttons to support gar ment when rolled on shoulder ; arm slings sewn down in cape ; leg slings to button inside skirts in front  Length to vary according to height of wearer

The provision of this garment is not compulsory and its wear is not obligatory in any order of dress, neither is it intended that the patterns must be rigidly followed as regards material or proofing process

**46 Whistles** —There is no sealed pattern, but all the officers of a unit should carry the same pattern.  They will be attached to a khaki cord or lan yard (R A leather strap) and carried in the left breast pocket of the khaki jacket, or they may be attached to a brace of the " Sam Browne " belt

### DECORATIONS AND MEDALS

**47 Method of Wearing** —Worn on the left breast of the full dress garment, over the sash in Highland and Scottish regiments, and under the pouch belt where this is worn  They are to be worn in a horizontal line suspended from a single bar or buckle, which is not to be seen, or stitched to the garment, and placed midway between the first and second buttons from the bottom of the collar, in Hussar regiments immediately below the top bar of lace on the left breast of the tunic

Medals are worn in the order of the dates of the campaigns for which they have been conferred  the first obtained being placed farthest from the left shoulder

Medals awarded by the Royal Humane Society or by the Royal National Life Boat Institution will, when authorized, be worn, in a position corresponding with war medals, on the right breast

When the decorations and medals cannot, on account of their number, be suspended from the bar so as to be fully seen, they are to overlap

Medals are to be worn so as to show the Sovereign's head

The first earned clasp should be worn nearest the medal

48  **Miniature Decorations and Medals** —Worn with mess dress and with evening dress (plain clothes) as directed in para 54  To be worn on the lapel in one horizontal line

Miniature decorations will be of the same size as miniature medals  A Knight Grand Cross, Knight Grand Commander, Knight Commander, or Commander will wear the miniature of the companionship or membership of the order  When the miniatures of the order of the Bath or of St Michael and St George are worn by a Knight Grand Cross or by a Knight Commander the buckle will be omitted

The miniatures of companionship or membership of an order will not be removed when in evening dress (plain clothes), the broad riband, star or badge is worn by a Knight Grand Cross, Knight Commander, etc

49  **Ribands of Decorations and Medals** —

**Full Dress.** —The riband is not to exceed 1 inch in length unless the possession of clasps requires it to be longer  The uppermost clasp to be 1 inch below the top of the riband  The buckles attached to the ribands of the third class of the orders of the Bath, and St Michael and St George, should show half way between the upper and lower edge of the riband

**Undress** —Ribands will be ½ inch in length, and will be sewn on to the cloth of the coat or jacket, or with white or khaki uniform worn on a bar without intervals, in the same position as prescribed for decorations and medals  They should not overlap, and when there is not sufficient room to wear the ribands in one row they should be worn in two or more rows, the lower being placed half-an inch below the upper  Ribands are not to be worn with the pea jacket

STARS OF ORDERS will be worn :—

In review order (staff in blue)

In evening dress (plain clothes) as directed in para 54

All stars of orders are to be worn in review order ; and in evening dress (plain clothes) as directed in para 54

The star of the senior order or decoration only will be worn in review order (staff in blue), unless it be desired to compliment a member of a particular order when the star of that order may be substituted

The stars of foreign orders will be worn on the right or left breast according to the regulation laid down by the Sovereign by whom they are conferred

In foreign countries British officers will wear their stars when foreign officers wear theirs

50  **Ribands and Badges of Orders** —On State occasions Knights Grand Cross and Knights Grand Commanders of any British Orders except the orders of the Garter and of the Thistle, will, when in review order or in evening dress (plain clothes), wear the broad ribands of the orders over the right shoulder, and under the sash or belt  The ribands of the orders of the Garter and the Thistle are worn over the left shoulder  Knights Commanders and Commanders will, when in review order, or in evening dress (plain clothes), wear the ribands of the order inside the collar of the tunic or coat, the badge being suspended two inches below the lower edge of the collar  Badges or orders are not to be worn except as above

In review order Knights Commanders of two or more orders will wear round the neck the riband and badge of the senior order, and may also wear the ribands and badges of one or more of the other orders  In evening dress (plain clothes) only the ribbon and badge of the senior order will be worn

On collar days the Knights Grand Cross and Knights Grand Commanders of the several orders wear the collar and badge and the star  The collar is worn under the shoulder cords and over the aiguillette  It is fastened to the shoulder cords by bows of white satin riband 1½ inches wide, and arranged so as to hang equally at back and front  When the collar is worn, the ribands and badges of the same order will not be worn  The collar is never worn after sunset  In the case of a Knight possessing two or more collars only one collar is worn at a time

The following are collar days :—

Easter Sunday, Monday and Tuesday

Ascension Day.

Whit Sunday, Monday and Tuesday

Trinity Sunday

| | | | |
|---|---|---|---|
| January | 1st | | New Year's Day |
| , | 6th | | Twelfth Day |
| February | 2nd | | Candlemas Day |
| ,, | 24th | | St Matthias |
| March | 1st | | St David |
| ,, | 17th | | St Patiick |
| , | 25th | | Lady Day |
| April | 23rd | | St Geoige |
| ,, | 25th | | St Mark |
| May | 1st | | St Philip and St James |
| , | 6th | | The King's Accession |
| ,, | 26th | | Queen Mary's Birthday |
| , | 29th | | Restoration of Royal Family |
| June | 3rd | | The King s Birthday |
| ,, | 22nd | | The King s Coronation |
| ,, | 24th | | St John the Baptist |
| ,, | 29th | | St Peter |
| July | 25th | | St James |
| August | 24th | | St Bartholomew |
| September | 21st | | St Matthew |
| ,, | 29th | | St Michael and All Angels |
| October | 18th | | St Luke |
| ,, | 28th | | St Simon and St Jude |
| November | 1st | | All Saints |
| ,, | 30th | · | St Andrew |
| December | 1st | | Queen Alexandra's Biithday |
| ,, | 21st | | St Thomas. |
| ,, | 25th | | Christmas Day |

Collars are also worn when His Majesty opens or prorogues Parliament

In undress the broad ribands of a Knight Grand Cross, Knight Giand Commander, Knight Commander, or Commander of an order aie not worn. The small riband of the companionship or membership of the order is worn on the left breast

**51 State, Official oi Public Occasions** —It will be considered a State occasion when the Sovereign, or the representative of the Sovereign, is piesent ; the parade in celebration of the birthday of the Sovereign ; or when specially oidered on the occasion of any parade, ceremony, or entertainment at which a member of the Royal Family is present

A function or entertainment given or arranged by any government depart ment or government institution will be regarded as an official occasion

When invitations are issued in the name of any municipal corporation, institu tion, society, or livery company, it will be regarded as a public occasion

**52 Order in which Decorations and Medals are to be worn** —Decorations and medals and their ribands will be worn in the following order :—

Victoria Cross.
*Order of the Garter
*Order of the Thistle
*Order of St Patrick
Order of the Bath
†*Order of Merit
Order of the Star of India.
Order of St Michael and St Geoige
Order of the Indian Empire
Royal Victorian Order
Distinguished Service Order
Imperial Service Order
Royal Victorian Order (Fifth Class)
Order of British India

---

\* These orders are not worn in miniature.
† Order of Merit comes immediately after G C B and is to be worn round the neck on all occasions

*Indian Order of Merit    (Military )
Kaisar i hind Medal
Order of St John of Jerusalem in England
Queen Victoria's Jubilee Medal, 1887 (Gold, Silver and Bronze)
Queen Victoria's Police Jubilee Medal, 1887
Queen Victoria s Jubilee Medal, 1897 (Gold, Silver and Bronze)
Queen Victoria's Police Jubilee Medal, 1897
Queen Victoria s Commemoration Medal, 1900 (Ireland)
King Edward s Coronation Medal
King Edward's Police Coronation Medal
King Edward's Durbar Medal (Gold, Silver and Bronze)
King s Medal, 1903 (Ireland)
King George s Coronation Medal
King George's Police Coronation Medal
King's Visit Commemoration Medal, 1911 (Ireland)
King George's Durbar Medal (Gold, Silver and Bronze)
Medal for Distinguished Conduct in the Field (Military)
Conspicuous Gallantry Medal (Naval)
Conspicuous Service Cross (Naval)
War Medals (in order of date)
Arctic Medal, 1815 1855
Arctic Medal, 1876
Antarctic Medal, 1901 1903
Constabulary Medal (Ireland)
Albert Medal.
Board of Trade Medal for Saving Life at Sea
*Indian Order of Merit (Civil)
Edward Medal
Indian Distinguished Service Medal
King s Police Medal
Long Service and Good Conduct Medal
Naval Long Service and Good Conduct Medal
Medal for Meritorious Service
Indian Long Service and Good Conduct Medal (for Europeans of Indian Army)
Indian Meritorious Service Medal (for Europeans of Indian Army)
Royal Marine Meritorious Service Medal
Indian Long Service and Good Conduct Medal (for Indian Army)
Indian Meritorious Service Medal (for Indian Army)
Volunteer Officers' Decoration
Volunteer Long Service Medal
Volunteer Officers' Decoration for India and the Colonies
Volunteer Long Service Medal for India and the Colonies
Colonial Auxiliary Forces Officers' Decoration.
Colonial Auxiliary Forces Long Service Medal
Medal for Good Shooting (Naval)
Militia Long Service Medal
Imperial Yeomanry Long Service Medal
Territorial Efficiency Medal
Territorial Decoration
Special Reserve Long Service and Good Conduct Medal
Decoration for Officers of the Royal Naval Reserve
Decoration for Officers of the Royal Naval Volunteer Reserve
Royal Naval Reserve Long Service and Good Conduct Medal
Royal Naval Volunteer Reserve Long Service Medal
Union of South Africa Commemoration Medal
Royal Victorian Medal (Gold and Silver)
Imperial Service Medal.
Medal of the Order of St John of Jerusalem in England
Badge of the Order of the League of Mercy
Royal Victorian Medal (Bronze )

---

* The Indian Order of Merit (Military and Civil) is distinct from the Order of Merit instituted in 1902

Foreign Orders (in order of date)
Foreign Decorations (in order of date)
Foreign Medals (in order of date)
The above order of decorations applies to those of similar grades    The minia
ture decoration or riband representing the higher grade of a junior order will,
however, when worn with that representing the lower grade of a senior order, be
placed before the latter    For instance, the miniature or riband of the "Indian
Empire" when worn by a G C.I E, who is also a K C B will come before the
miniature or riband of the "Bath "

53    **Foreign Decorations and Foieign War Medals** —The rules governing
the wearing of British decorations also apply to Foreign decorations for which full
permission has been given    Foreign decorations for which private permission has
been given will be worn in review order, in mess dress, and in evening dress (plain
clothes) on the occasions specified in the lettei of authority only, on the left of
all decorations and medals    The ribands of such decorations will not be worn on
the breast in ieview order (staff in blue) nor in undress or service dress    The
star of such a decoration will only be worn in review order (staff in blue) when
specially diiected    Miniatures of such decorations will only be worn on the
occasions mentioned in the letter of authority when mess dress or evening dress
(plain clothes) is worn

Foreign medals, other than war medals, are governed by the same rules as
foreign decorations

A foreign war medal, the wearing of which has been sanctioned by His Majesty,
or its riband, or miniature, will be worn in all orders of dress in the same way as
British medals

54    **Decorations and Medals aie worn in the seveial orders of dress
and in evening diess (plain clothes)** as follows :—

(a) *Review Order* —Broad riband and badge of a Grand Cross
   All stars of orders and all decorations and medals—para 47
   Knights Commanders and Commanders of one order will wear the badge
      of that order round the neck, and Knights Commanders and Com
      manders of two or more orders will wear the badge of the senior
      order round the neck.   They may also wear the badges of one or
      more of the other orders
   When the collar is worn, the broad riband of the Grand Cross of the
      same order is not worn

(b) *Review Order (staff in blue)* —Small ribands of the width of the com
      panionship or membership of orders and of medals, half inch in
      length on the breast    The star of the senior orders only is usually
      to be worn to the left and just clear of the left hand side row of
      buttons, but when specially directed, the star of another order
      may be substituted    The riband and badge assigned to a Knight
      Grand Cross, Knight Giand Commander, Knight Commander
      or Commander of an order is not worn

(c) *Mess Dress* —Miniature decorations and medals will be worn  Miniature
      decorations will be of the same size as miniature medals,
      and Knights Grand Cross, Knights Grand Commanders, Knights
      Commanders, and Commanders will wear the miniature of the
      companionship or membership

(d) *Undress and Service Dress* —Small ribands, of the width of the com
      panionship or membership of orders and of medals half inch in
      length on the breast

(c) *Evening Dress ( plain clothes)* —Broad riband and badge of a Grand
      Cross, with star of the order, and stars of all other orders, on State,
      public and official occasions    Knights Commanders and Com
      manders of one order, of which the star is worn, will wear the
      badge of that order round the neck, and Knights Commanders
      and Commanders of two or more orders, of which the stars are
      worn, will wear the badge of the senior order only    Miniature
      decorations and medals on the lapel of the coat    Knights Grand
      Cross, Knights Commanders, etc., wear the same miniatures
      with evening dress as with mess dress, and do not remove the

miniatures of companionship or membership when the higher grade decoration is worn

The badge of a baronet of Nova Scotia will be worn in review order, (staff in blue) and in evening dress (plain clothes) when the stars of knighthood are worn

The Royal Red Cross will be attached to a dark blue riband edged red, of one inch width tied in a bow and worn on the left shoulder Lady Nurses entitled to the decoration will wear it on such occasions as officers wear decorations Ordinarily the riband without the cross will be worn.

When evening dress (plain clothes) is worn, orders decorations and medals will be worn as follows :—

(1) At all parties and dinners when any member of the Royal Family is present—riband, stars, and miniature decorations and medals will be worn.

(2) At all parties and dinners given in the houses of Ambassadors and Ministers accredited to the Court of St James'—riband, stars and miniature decorations and medals will be worn The decoration of the country concerned should be worn in preference to the English one, and if both are worn, the former should take precedence of the latter

For informal or private dinners at an embassy or legation, when the Ambassador or Minister does not wish decorations to be worn, the Ambassador or Minister will be asked to make a notification to that effect on the invitation card

(3) On official occasions at the house of the Lord Lieutenant of a county within his county, and at all parties and dinners given by the Lord Mayor at the Mansion House and Guildhall—riband, stars, and miniature decorations and medals will be worn

(4) At all parties and dinners of an official nature given in the houses of Cabinet Ministers, Ex Cabinet Ministers, Knights of the Garter, Knights of the Thistle, Knights of St Patrick, or Great Officers of the Household—stars, not riband*, will be worn

(5) At all official dinners and receptions, including those of the City Livery Companies and City Corporations, regimental dinners, official naval dinners and all public dinners given in aid of charitable institutions—stars not riband,* will be worn

(6) At unofficial dinner parties or evening receptions in private houses, Knights of the Garter, Knights of the Thistle, or Knights of St Patrick should wear a star only

(7) The above are the only occasions on which decorations and medals will be worn with evening dress

The foregoing instructions apply to retired officers, and as regards the wearing of decorations and medals in review order, they also apply to white uniform when worn as full dress

---

* The expression 'stars, not riband means—
For Knights Grand Cross—stars, no riband
For members of the Order of Merit—badge and riband round the neck
For Knights Commanders—stars, no badge round the neck
For C. V. Os —badge and riband round the neck
For all classes—miniature medals and decorations

## ORDERS OF DRESS

55   The ordeis of dress are applicable to British Officers    Indian Officers will conform as far as possible :—

### REVIEW ORDER
## No 1—Full Dress

| DRESS | OCCASIONS WHEN WORN |
|---|---|
| Belt and Sword.<br>Full diess headdress and tunic or kurta with kamarband<br>Gloves or gauntlets<br>Sash or pouch belt<br><br>*Mounted*<br>Boots, Butcher<br>Pantaloons<br><br>*Dismounted*<br>Trousers.<br>Boots Wellington | (*a*) State ceremonies para 51<br>(*b*) Royal escorts<br>(*c*) Guards on Royal residences<br>(*d*) Guards of honour<br>(*e*) General courts martial<br>(*f*) Church parades<br>(*g*) Funerals.<br>(*h*) Ceremonies and entertainments when it is considered desirable to do special honour to the occasion   Official or public balls  dinners, luncheons oi bieakfasts and evening receptions as may be spe cially ordered |

The order of dress—Review order staff in blue (para. 81)—is applicable only to general officers and staff officers (para 83), and to heads of departments (if holding the substantive rank of colonel) at the head quarters of divisions (para 84)

When the order of dress is staff in blue, general officers will wear the frock coat ; staff officers and heads of departments (if hold ing the substantive rank of Colonel) will wear the frock coat or serge frock

Helmets are not taken to levées or balls in India

Officers of Indian cavalry wearing the kurta at levées will appear in Review order mounted and will not remove the lungi When attending General Courts Martial church parades and funerals they may wear Undress Order No 5, with full dress headdress.

Officers of Indian infantry dismounted on ceiemonial parades may wear pantaloons with ankle boots and putties or leggings without spurs, instead of trousers with Wellington boots, if more in conformity with the diess of their men

### HOT WEATHER—White

| | |
|---|---|
| Belt and Swoid.<br>Full dress headdress and white frock<br>Pouch belt<br>Waist sashe are not worn<br><br>*Mounted*<br>Boots, Butcher.<br>Pantaloons cloth<br><br>*Dismounted*<br>Trousers, white<br>Boots, Wellington | In hot weather on the occasions mentioned in No 1 Full Dress<br><br>Officers of the Indian Army do not wear this uniform when parading with their men |

| DRESS | OCCASIONS WHEN WORN |
|---|---|

### HOT WEATHER—Khaki

| | |
|---|---|
| Helmet khaki    Red, blue, or khaki lungi for Indian Cavalry wearing the kurta | By Officers of the British Service when specially ordered. |
| Jacket, or kurta with red, blue, or khaki kamarband | By British Officers of the Indian Army in hot weather on the occasions mentioned in No 1 |
| Sword ; Belt, " Sam Browne ' | Full Dress |
| *Mounted* | |
| Breeches, khaki ; white may be worn with the kurta. | |
| Boots—Butcher ; or ankle with putties or leggings.   Black or brown according to the colour of the putties worn by the men | |
| *Dismounted* | |
| Breeches with putties or leggings ;  or trousers with Wellington or ankle boots | |

### MARCHING ORDER

## No 2—Service Dress

| | |
|---|---|
| Boots, ankle with putties or leggings | (a) Field service |
| Breeches or knickerbockers | (b) Training |
| Field glasses or telescope | (c) Manœuvres |
| Gloves or gauntlets (if ordered) | (d) Marches |
| Great coat, (if ordered) | (e) Inspections |
| Havresack | |
| Helmet, or lungi ; khaki | |
| Jacket, or kurta and kamarband | |
| Sword ; Belt, " Sam Browne " | |
| Water bottle | |
| Whistle | |
| *On Field Service* | |
| First field dressing and identity disc | |
| Pistol and ammunition pouch | |

### DRILL ORDER

## No 3—Service Dress

| | |
|---|---|
| As in No 2 —Service Dress, with the following exceptions :— | (a) Divisional and brigade parades as may be ordered |
| Trousers may be worn when dismounted | (b) District courts martial, station boards, committees and courts of enquiry. |
| Field glasses or telescope, havresack, and water bottle will not be carried unless ordered | (c) Regimental courts martial and boards |
| | (d) All ordinary parades riding school and regimental duties |

### MESS ORDER

## No 4—Mess Dress (including White)

| | |
|---|---|
| Jacket | (a) When dining at Naval and Military messes. |
| Waistcoat (or kamarband in hot weather if worn) | (b) At Naval and Military evening entertainments and dances. |
| Overalls | (c) When dining with H E the Viceroy, the Governors of Madras, Bombay and Bengal, the C. in C, the Lieutenant Governor of a Province or when specially invited to meet these officers ; with a G O. C or Flag Officer of the Navy |
| Wellington boots | |
| Cloth overalls may be worn with the white jacket and white waistcoat or kamarband if desired regimentally | (d) Masonic balls    Officers who are Masons, wearing Masonic insignia, may wear plain clothes |
| | (e) As may be ordered |
| | (f) Will not be worn at manœuvres |

## UNDRESS ORDER
## No. 5—Undress

| DRESS | OCCASIONS WHEN WORN |
|---|---|
| Full dress helmet with spike and chain, or forage cap<br>Frock coat, or serge frock<br>White gloves (Regiments dressed in green or drab—Black or brown)<br>Trousers<br>Wellington boots<br>Full dress sword belt sash or girdle (with the frock coat).<br>Web belt with full dress slings worn under the serge frock, without sash, girdle or pouch belt<br>Swords will be worn on duty, and as occasion may require when not on duty | At afternoon Naval and Military dances and receptions in garrison or on board naval ships<br>At official interviews if uniform is ordered<br>On all other occasions when not on duty with troops for which no special order of dress is prescribed |

### HOT WEATHER

| | |
|---|---|
| Same as No 1, Full Dress—Hot Weather—White, but without medals, or pouch belt | As above, in the hot weather |

(1) The articles of dress mentioned in the above tables do not apply to officers of units for whom equivalent articles of different patterns are laid down in the detailed description of their uniforms (e g , Highland Regiments)

(2) In cases where alternative articles of uniform are allowed—e g , ankle boots and leggings instead of butcher boots—all officers of a unit must be dressed alike

56 **On Board Ship**—Service dress or undress (serge frock) and mess dress will be worn  The wearing of uniform by retired officers and Departmental officers with honorary rank returning to England on leave pending retirement is optional, but mess or evening dress will be worn at dinner

57 **On Field Service**—The articles of uniform required are detailed in the Field Service Manuals of units

58 **Horse Furniture**—Officers' horse furniture will include the head rope in all orders of parade  On field service and when specially ordered, mess tins, nose bags, picketing gear, horse's blanket, grass nets and surcingle pads will be carried

| Branch of Service | Review Order | Marching Order | Drill Order |
|---|---|---|---|
| Staff | Saddle Bridle complete Wallets (general officers wear the gold lace flounce over the wallets and the saddle-cloth, except when "Staff in blue" is the order of dress). Great coat when ordered carried behind the saddle Shoe case | As for review order, but without gold lace cover, flounce, and saddle cloth, for general officers Great coat rolled behind saddle Nose bag | As for marching order, but without great coat or nose bag |
| Cavalry | Saddle Bridle complete Wallets Leopard or lamb skin if worn Throat plumes The great-coat to be carried behind the saddle when ordered Shoe case | As for review order no leopard or lamb skin or throat plume Great coat rolled behind saddle Nose bag | As for marching order but without great coat or nose bag ; |
| Royal Artillery | As for cavalry | As for cavalry | As for cavalry |

| Branch of Service | Review Order | Marching Order | Drill Order |
|---|---|---|---|
| Royal Engineers | As for infantry | As for infantry | As for infantry |
| Infantry | Saddle Bridle complete Throat plumes when authorised Wallets Great-coat behind the saddle when ordered Shoe case | As for review order, but with great-coat rolled behind saddle Nose bag | As for marching order but without great-coat or nose bag. |
| Army Remount Department. | As for cavalry | As for cavalry | As for cavalry |
| Supply and Transport Corps. Indian Medical Service, Military Accounts Department | As for infantry | As for infantry | As for infantry |

## PART II.

### PERSONAL APPOINTMENTS.

### Aides-de Camp,   Aides de Camp General,   Equerries,   Extra Equerries, Honorary Physicians and Honorary Surgeons to the King Emperor, Equerries to Queen Alexandra; the Prince of Wales and other members of the Royal Family

59. Uniform and distinctions as described in Dress Regulations for the Army, Part II, except that the white " Wolseley ' pattern helmet with plume as in para. 61, and white uniform will be worn in India as occasion requires

Officers of the Indian Army who are appointed extra equerries to H R H the Prince of Wales will wear the aiguillette, laid down for equerries in the Dress Regulations for the Army at the Viceregal Court in India, at all Courts elsewhere, and when they meet His Royal Highness.

The special aiguillette worn by Indian orderlies to His Majesty the King Emperor shall be retained by them on their return to India but shall only be worn at Durbars, and at functions at which His Excellency the Viceroy may be present, on the Sovereign's birthday parade in India, and on the 1st January Proclamation parade

The following is a description of this special aiguillette :—

Wire cord $\frac{1}{4}$ inch gold, with plait and cord loop in front, and same at back, the plaits ending in plain cord with gilt metal tags   The plaits and cords front and back are joined together by a short gold braid strap in which is worked a button hole   The aiguillette is attached to the right shoulder of the garment by a button placed under the outer end of the shoulder cord or strap   The long cord is looped up on the top or front cord and the short and long plaits are fastened together, and a small gold braid loop is fixed thereon to attach to the top button of the garment on the side on which the aiguillette is worn   The arm is passed between the front plait and cord and the back or long plait and cord

### Military Secretaries and Aides-de Camp to the Commander in Chief and General Officers Commanding Armies and Divisions

60   Uniform as described for Staff and Personal Appointments in para 76, et seq   Plume as in para 61

### Personal Appointments* to the Viceroy and Governor General of India

*Full Dress*

61  **Boots** —Wellington, patent leather

**Buttons.**—Burnished—As in Appendix I

**Embroidery.**—Gold, lotus leaf device

**Helmet.**—White, cork, Wolseley pattern, gilt spike

**Lace.**—Gold, oak leaf pattern

**Pagri** —White muslin

**Plume** —Red swan feathers, 7 inches long, drooping outwards, with white feathers under, reaching to the end of the red ones

**Sash** —Gold and crimson silk net ; plaited runner and fringe tassels of gold and crimson silk.

**Scabbard.**—Steel, with gilt mountings

**Spurs** —Brass

**Straps** —Blue cloth

**Sword** —Mameluke gilt hilt, with device of the Royal Cypher and Crown ; ivory grip, scimitar blade

**Sword Belt** —Russia leather, $1\frac{1}{2}$ inches wide, with slings 1 inch wide ; three stripes of gold embroidery on belt and slings ; a gilt hook to hook up the sword

**Sword Knot** —Gold and crimson round cord strap, with gold and crimson acorn

**Trousers.**—Blue cloth with $1\frac{3}{4}$ inch lace down the side seams

**Tunic** —Scarlet cloth with blue cloth collar and cuffs, the skirt 12 inches deep for an officer 5 feet 9 inches in height   On each side in front, 8 embroidered loops with device of lotus leaves, 5 of them with buttons above the waist, and 3

* Except Private Secretary who if a military officer wears his military uniform

without buttons below it   A similar loop on each side of the collar.   Round cuffs, 3 inches deep   A scarlet flap on each sleeve, with 3 embroidered loops and large buttons, each loop 1¾ inches long exclusive of the drop   A scarlet flap on each back skirt, 10 inches long and 2 inches wide, with 2 loops and buttons similar to those on the sleeve ; 2 buttons at the waist behind   A gold aiguillette the cord ⁱ⁸⁄₁₀ inch in thickness, on the right shoulder, and a gold cord twisted loop, with a small button on the left   The collar, cuffs, flaps, and back skirts edged with white cloth ¼ inch wide, and the skirts lined with white   Hooks and eyes in front   No shoulder straps or badges of rank

### Scarlet Undress

62  **Tunic** —The same as the dress tunic, except that there are straight single line loops of scarlet mohair cord, instead of gold embroidery and on the collar a straight single blue cord loop with a small button at each end exactly over the button of the shoulder cord ; small buttons on the cuffs

All other articles as in full dress

### For Mounted Duties (Scarlet Undress)

63  **Boots** —Butcher

**Pantaloons** —Blue  cloth, with  1¾ inch  scarlet  cloth  stripes  down  the side seams

**Spurs** —Brass, swan neck  brass foot chains and patent leather spur straps

### Blue Undress

64.  **Boots** —Wellington, patent leather

**Forage Cap.** —Universal pattern, band of scarlet cloth

**Frock Coat** —Blue cloth, single breasted  to button down the front with eight holes and buttons  eight single line loops of blue silk twist on each side of the breast ; a similar loop on each side of the collar  with a small button at the end of each exactly over the button of the shoulder cord   Plain cuffs with four holes and buttons to each   A flap on each skirt behind, with a button at the bottom   A gold (gimp cord undress) aiguillette the cord ¹⁰⁄₁₀ of an inch in thickness on the right shoulder, and a gold (gimp twisted) cord with  a small button on the left ; two buttons at the waist behind   The skirts lined with black   A pocket inside each skirt behind   A shoulder strap of twisted gold thread   No badges of rank

**Frock** —Serge universal, blue, as in para 25 with gorget patches as in para. 78

**Straps** —Blue cloth

**Sword, Scabbard, Sword Belt, Sword Knot, Sash, Spurs** —As in full dress

**Trousers** —Blue cloth, with scarlet stripes 1¾ inches  wide  down the side seams

### For Mounted Duties (Blue Undress)

65  **Pantaloons, Boots, Spurs** —As in scarlet undress

### Evening Undress

66  **Dress Coat** —Blue cloth; velvet collar   Breast faced with "Star of India ' blue silk, skirts lined with same ; gilt buttons  4 on each sleeve, 2 behind

**Waistcoat** —White  single breasted  3 gilt buttons

**Trousers** —Black  plain

### Horse Furniture

67  **Bridle.** —Universal pattern, with dark blue enamel brow band and rosettes

**Saddle** —Universal pattern  Appendix VI

**Saddle Cloth.** —Blue cloth  lined moleskin  laced all  round with one inch gold lace ; at each hind corner a " Star of India   Badge (Silver star), with gilt motto, and gold embroidery outside

### General Instructions

68  **Blue Undress (Frock Coat)** —Will be worn  at reviews  and  inspections when  H  E  the Viceroy  is present  on ordinary occasions by the  A  D  C  in attendance on the Viceroy  and at receptions of and visits to Indian Chiefs, where  Undress ' is stated in the programme

**Cocked Hat** —Will be worn with Full Dress or Frock Coat

**Evening Undress,**—Will be worn when dining at Government House, or at other houses, when in attendance on, or to meet the Viceroy ; also at the house of the C in C, and of the Governor or the Lieutenant Governor of a Presidency or Province within his government

**Forage Cap** —Will be worn with serge frock

**Full Dress** —Will be worn at levées drawing rooms, and all evening enter tainments where the staff appear in uniform, and on such State occasions as shall be specially ordered

**Gloves** —White kid will be worn on all occasions, except with the serge frock

**Helmets** —Will be worn on all outdoor duties as may be ordered  Plume will be worn with the helmet in full dress, gilt spike in undress.

**Hot Weather Uniform** —Will consist of a plain white patrol jacket with breast pockets, gilt buttons, with braiding on the sleeves only plain collar with white linen collar inside to show $\frac{1}{8}$ inch  Gold undress aiguillette on right shoulder, with gold twisted cord on left, plain white overalls, black leather straps  Gloves will not be worn

**Honorary Aides de-Camp.**—When in attendance on the Viceroy, will wear their ordinary uniform with a gold full dress aiguillette, the cord $\frac{10}{48}$ inch in thickness, on the right shoulder over their tunics  blue frock coats, or patrol jackets  In the case of Volunteer officers, a silver aiguillette will be worn  On State occasions only, honorary surgeons to the Viceroy shall wear in uniform a full dress aiguillette, on the right shoulder, instead of a gold sash

**Scarlet Undress** —Will be worn on all mounted full dress duties

**Service Dress.**—Will consist of a khaki drill jacket and khaki covered helmet, khaki breeches, gaiters or brown jack boots, steel spurs, Sam Browne belt, brown doeskin gloves  Gorget patches as in para  27 will be worn on the collar of the frock

## Indian Aides de Camp to His Excellency the Viceroy

*(Except Gurkha officers who wear the same uniform as British officers of their regiments but with aiguillette )*

### Full Dress

69  **Aiguillette, Sword Belt and Knot**—As in para  61

**Boots** —Hessian

**Gloves** —White doeskin.

**Kamarband** —Blue with gold embroidered work

**Kurta** —Scarlet serge, to reach to knee  Body lined with scarlet Italian and sleeves with striped silesia  Open behind from waist to the bottom of skirt, the left skirt passing over the right by about $1\frac{3}{4}$ inches  Collar of blue cloth lined with black Italian $1\frac{3}{4}$ inches deep, square in front and fastened with 2 hooks and eyes.  Along the top and ends of the collar there is a row of lace (padded) with a row of gold braid eyes inside the lace  Cuffs pointed, of blue cloth $4\frac{3}{4}$ and $2\frac{1}{4}$ inches deep at the front and sides respectively  Along the top of the cuff there is a row of lace (padded on the top half of the sleeve only) the point extending to $6\frac{1}{2}$ inches from the cuff  Above the lace there is a row of gold braid eyes extending to $8\frac{1}{2}$ inches from the bottom of the cuff—below the lace there is a similar row of gold braid eyes except at the front where it is formed into a figurette; the latter reaches to the bottom of the cuff  A twisted gold shoulder cord on left side, the right side plain for aiguillette  Five large buttons down the front, the top one $1\frac{1}{4}$ inches from bottom of collar, the lowest 3 inches from waist seam  Two buttons on the waist seam behind, and a small one on the left shoulder for shoulder cord  On the waist seam of the left forepart there is a brass hook fastened to a loop of scarlet silk on the right side  There is a similar hook at the extreme point of the right skirt in front, fastened to a loop of scarlet silk on the inside of the left skirt  3 inches from the front to prevent the right skirt from drooping in front

**Lace** —Gold, oak leaf, $\frac{3}{4}$ inch

**Lungi.** —Blue with gold edging

**Pantaloons** —White cloth reaching to within 5 inches from the ground, opening at the bottom of the side seam for 7 inches, fastened with three small pearl buttons  White bone brace and fly buttons at the top  Large strappings of body cloth reaching to within $10\frac{1}{2}$ inches from the top and 8 inches from the bottom of the pantaloons  Two cross pockets

**Pouch** —The flap is pointed, and made of leather covered with blue cloth, and lined with red morocco leather 7 inches long and 5¼ inches broad at the bottom gradually widening to 6 inches broad at the top The edge of the flap is braided with lace gold ½ inch, oak leaf pattern A badge, gold embroidered Royal and Imperial Cypher with Crown above, and the motto "DIEU ET MON DROIT on two scrolls underneath to be placed on the front of the flap The pocket is made of tin 2 inches deep and 5¼ inches broad and covered with red morocco leather, a brass stud at the bottom for fixing flap The pouch is attached to the belt by gilt metal dees with swivels

**Pouch Belt** —Of red morocco leather 2⅝ inches wide of the length required tapering off to a tab 3 inches long at each end with button hole 1 inch from end of each tab, which is fastened back to a brass stud 4¼ inches from the end of each tab The outside of the belt is covered with gold lace, oak leaf pattern, 2½ inches wide the ends of the lace to be finished off at the end of each button hole

**Scabbard.**—Steel

**Sword** —Regimental pattern of the corps to which the officer belongs

**Spurs.**—Brass, jack, with foot chains

### Blue Undress

70 **Aiguillette** —As in para 64

**Blouse** —Blue serge, similar to Full Dress except that black mohair lace and braid is used instead of gold and the body is lined with black Italian

**Kamarband** —Red Cashmere

Other articles as in Full Dress

### Hot Weather Uniform

71 **Frock Coat** —White drill reaching to the knee opening at the back skirt of 18 inches Plain stand up collar 1¼ inches in depth, square at front and fastened with two hooks and eyes

Cuff formed with lace, white, 1⅛ inches The point of the lace 5 inches from bottom of cuff The lace is traced on both sides with white braid forming an Austrian knot above and below Five large buttons down the front

On the waist seam of the right forepart there is a metal button which fastens to a small rab on the left side One hook at the extreme point of the right skirt which fastens to an eye 3 inches from the front of the left skirt

**Pyjamas.**— White cotton, Jodhpur pattern, with a draw of string of white cotton tape

**Socks** —White cotton silk finish

**Shoes** —Patent leather (English)

### Personal Appointments * to the Governors of Madras and Bombay
#### Madras

72. Uniform as described for Staff and Personal Appointments in para 76 *et seq* Plume as in para 61 The aiguillette is worn on the right shoulder

### Evening Undress

**Dress Coat** —Blue cloth ; velvet collar: breast faced with yellow silk gilt buttons, 4 on each breast, 4 on each sleeve, and 2 behind

**Waistcoat** —White, with 3 gilt buttons

**Trousers** —Black, plain

#### Bombay

73 As above except that the dress coat is faced with primrose yellow silk

#### Madras and Bombay

74 † **Evening Undress** —Will be worn when dining at Government House or at other houses in attendance on, or to meet the Governor or G O C , Northern or Southern Armies Also at the houses of a Governor or Lieutenant Governor of a Presidency or Province, and of a G O C an Army within his Government or Command

**Frock** —The frock may be worn by the A D C in waiting within the precincts of Government House, and on parades when the officers of the army or divisional staff appear in that dress

---

* Except Private Secretary who if a Military officer wears his military uniform

† N B —This dress is not to be worn at private parties when the Governor is not present or at regimental messes or when on leave

**Full Dress.**—Will be worn at State reviews, levées, durbars, drawing rooms, State occasions when escorting Indian Chiefs, and at evening entertainments when so ordered.

**Helmets.**—Will be worn on all duties out of doors during the day

**White Uniform.**—The white frock with white trousers may be worn by the A D -C in waiting, during the hot weather

**Horse Furniture** —Horse furniture will be used on all mounted duties when belts and swords are worn

# PART III

## Field Marshals, General Officers, Substantive Colonels not belonging to a Corps or Department and Officers below the rank of Colonel not belonging to Corps or Departments extra regimentally employed

75 Uniform and horse furniture as described in Dress Regulations for the Army Brigadier Generals officiating as such may wear the uniform and appointments of their permanent rank or of the regiment or corps to which they belong, with the gorget patches of a General Officer or they may wear the uniform and appointments of a Brigadier General A staff officer appointed to officiate as Brigadier General will cease to wear the aiguillette while so officiating

# PART IV.

## STAFF AND PERSONAL APPOINTMENTS

## Officers of the Headquarter, General and Administrative Staffs and Officers holding Personal Appointments, not belonging to a corps or Department

76 The uniform and horse furniture of their rank with the following additions : —

**Aiguillette.**—Worn on the left shoulder with the tunic and frock coat Cord $\frac{1}{4}$ inch gold and red orris basket, with plait and cord loop in front and at back, the plaits ending in plain cord with gilt metal tags The plaits and cords, front and back, are joined together by a short scarlet cloth strap, in which is worked a button hole The aiguillette is attached to the shoulder of the tunic or frock coat by a button placed under the outer end of the shoulder cord The long cord is looped up on the top or front cord the front cord and the short and long plaits are fastened together, and a small gold braid loop is fixed thereon to attach to the top button of the tunic or the frock coat, on the latter on the side on which the aiguillette is worn The arm is passed between the front plait and cord and the back or long plait and cord

Aides de Camp to the King Emperor wear their special aiguillettes on the right shoulder

77 **Forage Cap and Badge** —*General Officers* universal pattern, blue cloth, scarlet band and welts, blue welt round crown, peak as in para 19 Badge, in gold embroidery on blue cloth the Royal Crest with Crossed sword and baton within a laurel wreath, blade of the sword in silver *Other Officers*, universal pattern, blue cloth with scarlet band and welts, blue welt round crown Peak as described in para 19 ; badge, the Royal Crest in gold embroidery on blue cloth

78 **Gorget Patches** —Worn on the collar of the serge frock

(a) General Officers of the headquarter staff, scarlet cloth $4\frac{1}{2}$ inches in length, pointed at the outer end, showing $\frac{3}{16}$ inch blue serge above and below the patch In the centre, a line of gold chain gimp $1\frac{3}{40}$ inch wide and $\frac{1}{8}$ inch deep A gorget button 1 inch from the point

(b) General Officers other than those of the headquarter staff, as above, except for a line of gold leaf embroidery along the centre of the patch in place of the line of gold chain gimp

(c) Officers below the rank of general officer, as above, but with crimson silk gimp instead of gold

79 **Service Dress.**—Jacket, as in para 31, with gorget patches as described in para 27, helmet, and breeches, universal pattern, boots and leggings, brown leather

**Officers of the Headquarter, General and Administrative Staffs, and Officers holding Personal Appointments belonging to a Corps or Department**

80 **Full Dress** —Full dress of unit, aiguillette as described in para 76 on the left shoulder   Aides de Camp to the King Emperor and officers of the Household Cavalry wear their special aiguillettes on the right shoulder   White Wolseley helmet with plume and chain

**Forage Cap and Badge** —As in para 77

**Great coat** —Universal pattern, drab, with shoulder straps edged with two broad stripes of red cloth, showing ½ inch of serge material between   Buttons regimental

**Horse Furniture** —Universal pattern   Appendix VI   Brow band and rosettes, regimental.

**Mess Dress** —Regimental

81. **Review Order, Staff in Blue**

*White Wolseley Helmet*, with gilt metal spike and chain

*Frock Coat* —Universal pattern as described in para 24, Staff Aiguillette   Buttons regimental   Officers of rifle regiments and regiments dressed in green and drab wear gilt burnished buttons with the Garter and motto surmounted by a crown ; within the Garter the Royal Cypher

*Pantaloons and Trousers.*—Blue cloth, with scarlet stripes 1¾ inches wide

*Sword Belt, Girdle, Waistsash, Dirk belt, and Slings* —Regimental pattern. Officers of rifle regiments and regiments dressed in green and drab wear a belt of Russia leather, 1½ inches wide, gold laced, staff pattern, with gold laced slings 1 inch wide, and lion head buckles   Waist plate, rectangular gilt burnished plate, bearing in silver, the Royal Cypher surmounted by a Crown, an oak branch on each side, and a scroll inscribed *"Dieu et mon droit"* below   Officers of Highland regiments wear the claymore attached by gold laced slings to the dees of the dirk belt

Staff Officers of the Indian Army, below the rank of general officer may wear their regimental serge frocks with gorget patches as in para 78 with other articles of their full dress regimental uniform as Review Order, Staff in Blue   The aiguillette and pouch belt are not worn with the serge frock

82 **Service Dress** —Regimental, with gorget patches as in para 27

## Staff Distinctions

83 Officers permanently holding the following appointments will wear Staff distinctions   These distinctions are the aiguillette with tunic and frock coat, the gorget patch on the serge frock and service dress jacket, the forage cap (para 77 and the order of dress " Review order—staff in blue " :—

(1) Officers of the Army Department
(2) Staff Officers at Army Head quarters, India (para 287, A R, I, Vol II)
(3) Inspector of Cavalry
    Inspector of R H and R F A
    Inspector of R G A
    Inspector of Volunteers.
(4) Officers of the General Staff.
    Deputy—, Assistant—, and Deputy Assistant Adjutant General
    Deputy—, Assistant—, and Deputy Assistant Quartermaster General
    Brigade Major
    Staff Captain
    Station Staff Officer, 1st Class
(5) Military and Assistant Military Secretary
    Aide de Camp
    Military Attaché

Officers holding appointments at training and manœuvres, which on active service would be permanent staff appointments (e g , Staff Captain of Brigade) will wear gorget patches in service dress

84 The following heads of services and departments (if holding the substantive rank of Colonel) may wear the frock coat (in Indian Army the serge frock is

permissible) in place of the tunic when the order of dress is " Review order—staff in blue "

    Commanding Royal Engineer
    Director or Deputy Director of Ordnance Factories.
    Director or Assistant Director of Ordnance Inspection
    Assistant Director of Transport
    Assistant Director of Supplies
    Deputy or Assistant Director of Medical Services of Divisions
    Inspecting Veterinary Officer

# PART V.

## BRITISH ARMY

85  Officers on the Indian Establishment :—

Uniform and horse furniture as described in Dress Regulations for the Army For the convenience of officers who may not have easy access to that book much of the detail contained therein is reproduced in these regulations, but it is to be understood that the principle of complying with Dress Regulations for the Army is to be strictly adhered to.

Officers will conform in details of their dress to such special orders as may be applied to the uniform of their men in India, and deviations from Dress Regulations for the Army which are not in accordance with such orders are not to be permitted

The white frock described in these regulations is the universal pattern for all officers in India

The Orders of Dress in these regulations are applicable to all officers

# PART VI

## VICEROY'S BODYGUARD

### British Officers

*Full Dress*

86  **Boots** —Mounted —Napoleon, patent leather

Dismounted —Wellington, patent leather

**Buttons** —As in Appendix I

**Cloak and Cape** —Blue cloth to reach the ankles when worn on foot, scarlet shalloon lining, gilt buttons of regimental pattern, shoulder straps of the same material as the cloak with small button at the top  Badges of rank in gold on the shoulder straps

**Embroidery** —Gold lotus leaf device

**Gauntlets** —White leather

**Girdle** —Gold lace, 2½ inches wide, with 2 crimson stripes, on scarlet morocco leather.

**Helmet** —White, cork, cavalry pattern, with spike of bright gilt metal of regimental pattern, gilt base, leaf pattern

**Lace** —Gold oak leaf pattern

**Pagri** —White muslin

**Pantaloons.**—White, melton cloth

**Pouch.**—Gold embroidery and gold braid on blue cloth, and blue morocco leather, gilt ends and buttons

**Pouch Belt** —Gold oak leaf lace on scarlet morocco leather, gilt buckle tips, side prickers and chains

**Sabretache** —Gold embroidery and gold oak leaf lace on scarlet cloth, and scarlet morocco leather, gilt rings and buckles and gold oak leaf lace slings

**Scabbard.**—Steel

**Spurs.**—Mounted —Silver plated, swan neck, to buckle with strap and foot chains

Dismounted.—Brass, box

**Sword.**—Cavalry pattern

**Sword Belt** —White web with sword suspender and gold lace slings and gilt buckles

**Sword Knot.**—Gold round cord with gold acorn

**Trousers.**—Blue cloth with one and three quarter inch lace down the side seams   Black leather foot straps

**Tunic** — Scarlet cloth, with blue collar and cuffs; the skirt 12 inches deep for an officer 5 feet 9 inches in height   On each side in front, 8 straight loops of scarlet mohair cord, 5 of them with buttons above the waist and 3 below it   Embroidered loops with device of lotus leaves on the collar   Round cuffs 3 inches deep. A scarlet flap on each sleeve with 3 buttons   A scarlet flap on each back skirt, 10 inches long and 2 inches wide, with 2 buttons similar to those on the sleeve ; 2 buttons at the waist behind.   A gold aiguillette, the cord $\frac{1}{8}$ inch in thickness on the right shoulder and a gold chain gimp plaited shoulder strap lined with scarlet, on the left shoulder   Badges of rank in silver embroidery on the left shoulder strap   The collar cuffs, flaps and back skirts edged with white cloth, $\frac{1}{4}$ inch wide, and the skirt lined with white   Hooks and eyes in front

**Tunic, Riding**—The same as the full dress tunic, except that on the collar there are straight single line loops of scarlet mohair cord with a small button at each end exactly over the button of the shoulder strap

*Undress Blue*

**87  Aiguillette** —The same pattern as the undress aiguillette for Personal Appointments—para. 64

**Boots** —Mounted —Butcher

Dismounted —Wellington, plain black leather

**Field Cap** —Blue cloth, folding, 5 inches in height, with scarlet cloth top ; blue side flaps 4 inches deep, to turn down when required   Gold French braid welts on cap and flaps and at front and back seams   Badge at the left side

**Forage Cap** —Blue, gold oak leaf lace with Lancer quarterings   Worn only with the frock coat   In other orders of dress the cap for Personal Appointments is worn—para 64

**Frock Coat** —Blue cloth, trimmed with black braid, regimental pattern ; a shoulder strap of blue cloth on the left shoulder, edged with $\frac{1}{2}$ inch black mohair braid, except at the base, black netted button at top, badges of rank in gold on the left shoulder strap.   The undress aiguillette is worn on the right shoulder

**Frock Serge, Universal** —As in para 25 ; straight single line loops of scarlet mohair cord on the collar, with a small button at each end, exactly over button of the shoulder strap

**Gloves** – White leather with frock coat ; brown with serge frock

**Helmet** —As in full dress

**Pantaloons** —Blue cloth, with scarlet stripes $1\frac{1}{4}$ inches wide down the side seams

**Sabretache** —Black enamelled leather, with brown leather slings and brass buckles

**Spurs.**— As in full dress

**Sword and Scabbard** —As in full dress

**Sword Belt** —As in full dress

**Sword Knot** —Brown leather strap

**Trousers**—Blue cloth, with scarlet stripes, $1\frac{3}{4}$ inches wide down the side seams   Black leather foot straps

*Mess Dress*

**88  Boots** —Wellington, patent leather

**Mess Jacket** —Scarlet cloth of regimental pattern, with blue cloth collar and cuffs trimmed with gold lace, shoulder straps and badges of rank as for tunic

**Mess Waistcoat** —Blue cloth of regimental pattern, trimmed with gold lace.

**Spurs** —Brass, box, regimental pattern

**Trousers** —As in full dress

*Hot Weather Uniform— White*

**9**  As in para  30 : but the frock has blue piping round the bottom of the collar, on the cuffs, up the back sleeve and body seams   Shoulder titles are not worn. In full dress the aiguillette as for the tunic and in undress as for the frock coat is worn. In drill order neither aiguillette is worn.

The white mess jacket is piped as above and has a stand up collar fastened with 3 hooks and eyes. White linen collar and black tie are not worn. The kamarband is blue silk.

*Horse Furniture*

90  **Bridle** —Universal pattern. As in Appendix VI

**Chain Reins** —Steel

**Girths** —Dark blue

**Leopard Skin** —Gold fringe and scarlet edging

**Saddle** —Universal pattern. As in Appendix VI

**Shabraque** —Blue cloth, with gold oak leaf lace and gold embroidery regimental pattern

**Throat Ornament** —Red

### Indian Officers

91  **Aiguillette** —In full dress the same as the full dress of His Excellency the Viceroy's Personal Appointments, in undress of a similar pattern to that for the Personal Appointments, but of worsted instead of gold thread

**Boots** —Napoleon, patent leather

**Cloak** —Regulation cavalry pattern, badges of rank in gilt metal

**Frock Coat** —Scarlet cloth, fastened with buttons of regimental pattern in front, blue facings and lancer piping ; gold embroidery round neck and in front, regimental pattern ; sleeves, gold lace double lancer pattern raised. Plated, shoulder chains, with badges of rank in gilt metal

**Gauntlets** —White leather

**Girdle** —Gold lace, 2½ inches wide, with 2 crimson stripes

**Lungi** —Blue and gold ; kullah red and gold

**Pantaloons** — { Full Dress—White cloth
{ Undress—Blue cloth

**Pouch and Pouch Belt** —As for British officers

**Spurs.**—Swan neck with foot chains, silver plated

**Sword and Scabbard** —Straight regulation Cavalry, steel scabbard with rings for full dress and black leather scabbard for undress

**Sword Belt** —Gold lace girdle, with gold lace slings

**Sword Knot** —Gold line with acorn

*Horse Furniture*

92  As for British officers except :—

**Shabraque** —Blue cloth, with oak leaf pattern gold lace edging. No embroidery

### British Officers

*Full Dress*

93  **Boots** —Mounted —Butcher
               Dismounted —Wellington

**Cap Lines** —Gold wire

**Cloak** —Regimental pattern

**Gloves** —White leather

**Helmet.**—Regimental pattern

**Lace** —Gold Vandyke pattern

**Pagri** —Regimental pattern

**Pantaloons** —White melton cloth

**Pouch Belt** —Gold Vandyke lace on blue morocco leather, silver buckle, tip slide, prickers and chains

**Pouch Box** —Lined blue morocco leather, with silver flap, as for Hussars.

**Spurs** —Mounted —Silver plated swan neck, to buckle with strap and foot chains

           Dismounted —Gilt box spurs

**Sword and Scabbard.**—Cavalry pattern

**Sword Belt** —Gold Vandyke lace on blue morocco leather, gilt buckles, snake fastening

**Sword Knot.**— Gold line with acorn

**Trousers.**—Blue cloth, with double gold Vandyke lace stripes.

**Tunic** —Scarlet cloth, Hussar pattern, with blue cloth collar and cuffs, trimmed as for Hussars with gold gimp. Shoulder cords of plaited gold chain gimp lined with scarlet   Badges of rank in silver embroidery

*Undress*

94  **Forage Cap** —Universal pattern, scarlet, blue band

**Frock Coat.**—Blue cloth, single breasted  The collar edged with $\frac{3}{4}$ inch black braid, and with figuring in narrow braid  A braided figure on each sleeve extending to 10 inches from the bottom of the cuff  Six loops of inch braid across the breast with four rows of olivets  The back seams and back skirts trimmed with inch braid, traced round with narrow braid, and with olivets and tassels  The skirts lined with black shoulder-straps of the same material as the garment, edged with $\frac{1}{2}$ inch black mohair braid, except at the base ; black netted button at the top; badges of rank in gilt or gilding metal

**Pantaloons.**—Blue cloth with double yellow stripes

**Patrol Jacket** —Hussar pattern

Other articles as in full dress  Pouch belt not worn

*Mess Dress*

95  **Mess Jacket** —Scarlet cloth, blue facings, regimental pattern trimmings

**Mess Waistcoat.**—Blue cloth, trimmed regimental pattern

**Trousers, Boots and Spurs** —As in full dress

*Hot Weather Uniform*

96  As in para 30

*Horse Furniture*

97  As for Hussars

**Shabraque** —Blue cloth, gold embroidery, regimental pattern

**Throat Ornament** —Red

## Indian Officers

98  **Alkhalak** —Scarlet cloth, gold Vandyke lace edging, $1\frac{1}{2}$ inches wide round neck, breast and cuffs ; gold tracing braid round skirts ; embroidered sleeves and steel shoulder chains on blue cloth

**Boots** —Napoleon

**Cloak** —Regimental pattern

**Gloves** —Buckskin

**Horse Furniture** —As for British officers

**Kamarband** —Scarlet, of Kashmir work

**Lungi.**— Blue and gold

**Pantaloons** —White moleskin

**Spurs.**—Swan neck, silver plated with foot chains

**Sword**  Regimental pattern

**Sword Belt** — ⎱ Buff
**Sword Knot** — ⎰

### GOVERNOR'S BODYGUARD BOMBAY.

## British Officers

*Full Dress*

99  **Cap Lines** —Lancer, gold, with acorns

**Cloak** —Regulation cavalry

**Boots** —Mounted —Knee, cut with a V at the top
         Dismounted —Wellington

**Gauntlets.**—White leather

**Girdle** —Gold lace, $2\frac{1}{2}$ inches wide, with 2 blue stripes on blue silk showing at edges

**Horse Furniture.**—As for Hussars

**Kurta** — Scarlet cloth, regimental pattern

**Lungi** —Red, with gold and blue ends

**Lace.**—Gold, Lancer pattern.

**Pantaloons** —Blue cloth, with double yellow cloth stripes showing blue light between   White leather for wear with the kurta

**Pouch** —Black patent leather, 6 inches by 2 inches ; silver buckles, gilt mountings

**Pouch Belt** —Gold lace on blue morocco leather, blue stripe in centre, silver buckles, slide and tip

**Spurs** —Mounted —Jack, crane necked
          Dismounted.—Box, regimental pattern

**Sword and Scabbard** —Cavalry pattern

**Sword Belt** —Blue web; slings, gold lace on blue morocco leather, gilt buckles

**Sword Knot.**—Gold line with acorn

**Trousers.**—Blue cloth, with double yellow cloth stripes

**Tunic** —Scarlet cloth, Lancer pattern, trimmed with gold lace blue lapel, blue piping to back seams of body and sleeves ; blue cloth collar and cuffs ; shoulder cords of plaited gold cord lined with scarlet ; badges of rank in silver embroidery.

*Undress*

100 **Forage Cap** —Universal pattern, scarlet band

**Frock Coat** —Regimental pattern ; badges of rank in gilt or gilding metal

**Frock** —Blue serge, regimental pattern

**Gloves** —Brown leather

**Sword Belt and Knot** —White buff leather

**Other** articles as in full dress   Pouch belt not worn

*Mess Dress*

101 Regimental Mess dress is worn

*Hot Weather Uniform*

102 As in para 30

## Indian Officers

103 **Frock Coat** —Scarlet cloth, blue lapel collar, cuffs and piping   Lacing and shoulder cords as for British officers' tunic

**Kurta** —Red serge or cloth, facings dark blue with tracing of gold lace on front and back regimental pattern

**Lungi** —Red, with gold and blue ends

**Scabbard** —Steel, with a large shoe at the bottom, and a trumpet shaped mouth

**Sword** —Half basket steel hilt, with two fluted bars on the outside black fish skin grip bound with silver wire ; slightly curved blade, 35 inches long and $1\frac{1}{4}$ inches wide at the shoulder, grooved and spear-pointed

**Horse Furniture** —As for British officers

Other articles as for British officers

## INDIAN CAVALRY AND LANCERS
### GENERAL
## British Officers

104  Applicable to all cavalry units except as stated in the following paras

**Boots**—As in para  16

**Forage Cap.**—As in para  19   Cap the colour of the  tunic or kurta ; band and  welts the colour of the facings.

**Frock,  Serge.**—As in para  25, or of the colour of  the uniform

**Gauntlets**—White leather    With the serge frock, white gloves

**Great coat.**—As in para  28, or regimental pattern

**Helmet.**—As in para 29

**H  W  Uniform,  Full dress.**—Khaki kurta  or jacket when on duty with the men    White (optional)  on other occasions, as in  para 30   In Lancer regiments the white frock has piping up the seams

**H  W  Mess Uniform.**—As in para 30   Lancers; piping as on the white frock

**Horse Furniture**—Universal pattern—As in Appendix VI

**Kurta and Tunic**—The kurta is worn in full dress by officers of Indian cavalry regiments, except the 23rd Cavalry  F  F ; the 26th, 27th, and 28th Light Cavalry and the Guides Cavalry, the  officers of which wear the tunic on all full  dress occasions

Except in the above named  regiments, the kurta will be worn on parade with the men and when in the presence of H  I  M  the King Emperor : on other full dress occasions officers in  possession of tunics may wear them.  In regiments which wear the kurta the purchase of tunics by officers on joining will  be strictly voluntary

Officers wearing the  kurta at levées will wear the lungi and will salute instead of bowing   At State balls the lungi will not be worn

Officers not in possession of tunics, when attending General Courts Martial, and in Church, may wear Undress Order No 5, as in para  55

**Lungi.**—Regimental pattern

**Mess Waistcoat**—Of blue or red cloth or of the colour of the facings, as may be desired regimentally, fastening up to the throat with hooks, and trimmed with $\frac{1}{2}$ inch lace, gilt studs down the front ; if desired regimentally an open white drill waistcoat with 4 small regimental buttons, to be worn with  collar and black tie

**Service Dress**—Universal pattern

**Sword and Scabbard**—As in Appendix VIII

**Spurs**—Steel spurs are worn  in all  orders  of  dress in regiments in which the men wear steel, and brass spurs in regiments in which the men wear brass

### 3rd SKINNER'S HORSE   5th, 6th  AND 12th  CAVALRY
## British Officers
*Full Dress*

105  **Gloves**—White leather

**Kurta, Lungi and Kamaiband**—Regimental  pattern

**Lace**—Light dragoon pattern

**Pantaloons.**—Blue diagonal cloth with stripes as on trousers   With the kurta, white melton cloth for regiments wearing white pyjamas in full dress; Bedford cord for those wearing drab or 'Multani' colour

**Pouch**—Of cloth  the  colour of the facings, $6\frac{1}{2}$ inches long  $2\frac{1}{4}$ inches wide, embroidered in gold, regimental pattern

**Pouch Belt**—Gold lace, $2\frac{1}{4}$  inches wide, to match sword belt, buckle, tip,  and slide of regimental pattern

**Sword Belt**—Gold lace, $1\frac{1}{2}$ inches wide, with slings 1 inch wide, on morocco leather  with edging of the colour of the facings, fastened in front with plate of regimental pattern   Slings fastened to the belt with two rings

**Sword Knot.**—Gold cord and acorn

**Trousers**—Blue cloth, a stripe the colour of the facings, $1\frac{1}{2}$ inches  wide, down the side seams   The 5th Cavalry wear scarlet and the 12th Cavalry double yellow stripes

**Tunic** (*Optional*) —Cloth the colour of the uniform of the regiment, with collar and cuffs of regimental facings ; single-breasted, edged all round, except the collar, with heavy Russia braid, R A Pattern   Collar laced all round the top with ¾ inch gold lace and one row of heavy Russia braid round the bottom seam   Breast ornamented with 5 rows of gold round back cord (staff pattern) and terminating with crow's feet and olivets, Hussar pattern   Each breast loop is formed of three cords plaited together and finished at each end with a gold olivet ; underneath is sewn a hook to pass through an eye sewn on the breast of the tunic at the inner side of the crow s foot ; the olivets to be disposed to hide joining   On each back seam a double line of gold flat plait braid terminating at the top with a crow's foot and ending in a figure reaching to the bottom of the skirt   A knot on each sleeve, traced and figured according to authorized patterns, nine inches high   The skirt rounded off in front, closed behind, and lined with black   Shoulder cords of plaited g ld chain gimp lined with cloth the colour of the tunic, badges of rank in silver embroidery

### Undress

106  **Frock** —As in para 25   Collar edged round with narrow Russia gimp   Regimental numerals and initials in brass on the shoulder straps

**Gloves.**—As in para 26

**Pantaloons** —Blue, as in full dress

Other articles as in full dress   Pouch belt not worn

### Mess Dress

107. **Mess Jacket** —Cloth or serge the colour of uniform, long-waisted coming to a point behind, cut round over the hips, fastening up to the throat with hooks, gilt studs down the front ; lace ½ inch wide   Shoulder straps of plain cloth of the colour of the jacket and edged with ½ inch lace   Collar and pointed cuffs, the colour of the facings   Badges of rank in gold embroidery   When worn open the jacket is fastened by a loop of tracing braid

**Trousers and Spurs** —As in full dress

### Horse Furniture

108  **Throat Ornament** —Worn in the following regiments :—3rd Skinner's Horse—Scarlet ; 6th Cavalry—Red and white

### 21st  22nd  23rd AND 25th CAVALRY
## British Officers
### Full Dress

109  **Kurta** —Regimental pattern (not worn in 23rd Cavalry)

**Lace.**—Gold, regimental pattern

**Pantaloons** —With the kurta, white melton cloth   On other occasions blue diagonal cloth (25th Cavalry—Rifle green) with stripes as on trousers

**Pouch** – Cloth the colour of the facings, 6½ inches × 2¼ inches embroidered in gold with device of regimental pattern   The 23rd Cavalry, pouch of blue cloth

**Pouch Belt** —Gold lace to correspond with sword belt, 2½ inches wide ; buckle, tip and slide of regimental pattern.

**Sword and Scabbard.**—As in Appendix VIII   The 25th Cavalry ; full dress sword and scabbard of regimental pattern

**Sword Belt** —Gold lace 2 inches wide, lined morocco leather the colour of the facings, fastened in front with regimental pattern plate of the same width as the belt ; two rings for sword slings ; slings of gold lace, 1 inch wide, lined as for belt, fastened with buckles and leather straps

**Sword Knot** —Gold line with acorn—25th Cavalry ; gold and red line with acorn

**Trousers** —Blue (25th Cavalry—green) cloth, with double red stripes ¾ inch wide and ¼ inch apart

**Tunic** — (*21st Cavalry Optional*) *23rd Cavalry* —Cloth of regimental colour, Hussar pattern with collar and cuffs of regimental facings ; edged all round, except collar, with gold cord ; collar laced round the top with ¾ inch gold lace and on the seam with one row of heavy Russia braid    Sleeves laced, an Austrian knot of gold cord on each sleeve reaching to 8 inches from the bottom of the cuff, and traced with plain gold braid, 5 quadruple rows of black cord hanging loose across the breast    Shoulder straps of plaited gold gimp, lined with cloth, the colour of the uniform, with a small gilt button at top; badges of rank in silver embroidery

### Undress

**110 Frock** —As in para 25
**Scabbard** —22nd and 25th Cavalry black leather scabbard
Other articles as in full dres    Pouch belt not worn

### Mess Dress

**111 Mess Jacket** —Cloth of regimental colour, long waisted coming to a point behind, cut round over the hips, fastening up to the throat with hooks, gilt studs down the front, lace $\frac{1}{2}$ inch wide    Collar and pointed cuffs of the colour of the facings    Shoulder straps of the same material and colour as the jacket, edged with $\frac{1}{2}$ inch lace    Badges of rank in gold embroidery

The jacket is worn open, fastened by a loop of tracing braid at the neck

**Trousers and Spurs** —As in Full Dress

### Hot Weather Uniform

112   The 21st, 22nd, 23rd and 25th Cavalry wear khaki at all times

### Horse Furniture

113   **Throat Ornament** —23rd and 25th Cavalry—Scarlet

**33rd LIGHT CAVALRY 34th POONA HORSE 35th SCINDE HORSE 36th JACOB'S HORSE**

## British Officers

### Full Dress

**114 Gauntlets.**—White buckskin
**Kamarband** —Red merino
**Kurta** —Serge, dark blue with collar the colour of the facings $1\frac{1}{2}$ inches high and rounded in front, one row of flat gold 1 inch lace round the top and bottom    Pointed cuffs the colour of the facings, $5\frac{1}{2}$ inches deep at the point and $1\frac{1}{4}$ inches at the back seam, ornamented with 1 inch lace round the top    Removable steel shoulder chains fastened on leather    (35th Horse—Red cloth) straps, with badges of rank in gilt or gilding metal, and crossed gilt tulwars, with numerals and initials of the regiment    The kurta is worn loose, open to the waist, and fastened with 4 round plain brass buttons, $\frac{3}{4}$ inch diameter; skirt, to reach to within two inches of the knee

**Lace** —Gold, zig zag pattern
**Pantaloons** —With the Kurta    White melton cloth, (34th Horse—White moleskin)    On other occasions—Blue diagonal cloth with stripes as on trousers
**Pouch** —Silver, $7\frac{1}{2}$" by $2\frac{3}{4}$", buckles silver, lined red morocco
**Pouch Belt** —$2\frac{1}{4}$ inches wide, double gold lace, $\frac{7}{8}$ inch wide, $\frac{1}{4}$ inch red silk stripe ; lined morocco ; buckles, tips, slides, whistle and chain, plain silver
**Sword Belt** —Double gold lace, 2 inches wide, with $\frac{1}{4}$ inch silk stripe in centre ; slings $1\frac{1}{4}$ inches wide with $\frac{1}{8}$ inch silk stripe in centre    Belt and slings lined with red morocco leather fastened with a gilt rectangular burnished plate.
**Sword Knot.**—Gold and red cord with gold acorn
**Trousers** —Dark blue cloth with a stripe the colour of the facings $1\frac{1}{2}$ inches wide, down the side seams
**Tunic** (*Optional*) —Cloth, dark blue with collar and cuffs of regimental facings    The collar ornamented with 1 inch lace round the top, and round back gold cord round the bottom    The cuffs pointed and edged with round back gold cord forming an Austrian knot, 7 inches deep    Eight buttons in front and 2 at the waist behind ; flap on each skirt behind with 3 buttons, edged with round back gold cord traced inside and out with gold Russia braid    Front of tunic edged with cloth the colour of the facings ; skirts lined with white    Gilt shoulder cords lined with blue    Badges of rank in silver embroidery

*Undress*

**115   Frock** —As in para 25
**Gloves** —As in para. 26
Other articles as in full dress   Pouch belt not worn

*Mess Dress*

**116   Mess Jacket** —Cloth, dark blue, long waisted ; coming to a point behind and cut round over the hips, edged all round including the collar with ½ inch gold lace ; collar and cuffs of regimental facings, the latter pointed with ½ inch lace ; gimp at base of collar   Double gold tracing braid on back seams, terminating at sleeves with treble eyes and at waist with two embroidered frogs ; gilt studs fastening with hooks down the front ; worn open at mess fastened by loop of tracing braid at the throat   Shoulder straps of cloth the colour of the jacket, and edged with ½ inch lace, (33rd Light Cavalry—Shoulder straps of gold cord), badges of rank in gold embroidery.

**Trousers and Spurs** —As in Full Dress

*Horse Furniture*

**117   Throat Ornaments** —

| | |
|---|---|
| 33rd Light Cavalry    • | Scarlet |
| 34th Poona Horse | French grey |
| 35th Scinde Horse | White |
| 36th Jacob s Horse | Primrose |

1st, 2nd LANCERS, 4th CAVALRY, 7th LANCERS, 8th CAVALRY, 9th HODSON'S HORSE 10th 11th 13th, 14th 15th LANCERS, 16th 17th CAVALRY 18th 19th LANCERS

### British Officers

*Full Dress*

**118   Cap Lines** —Gold with acorns ; 13th and 19th Lancers, silver
**Gauntlets.**—White leather
**Girdle.**—Gold or silver lace, 2½ inches wide, with two crimson (1st Lancers, black ; 7th Lancers, blue ; 19th Lancers, French grey) silk stripes, lined with morocco leather, the colour of the facings (18th Lancers—Red)
**Kurta** —Regimental pattern.
**Lace** —Gold (13th and 19th Lancers—Silver) Lancer pattern
**Pantaloons** —With the Kurta—White melton cloth or Bedford cord ; 10th Lancers—White velvet cord   On other occasions—Blue diagonal cloth with stripes as on trousers
**Pouch** —Scarlet leather (1st and 19th Lancers —Black ; 4th Cavalry and 13th Lancers—Silver ; 2nd and 18th Lancers—Blue) 6½ inches long and 2¾ inches broad with plated (1st and 10th Lancers—Silver) flap engraved ; device of regimental pattern   The 11th Lancers, pouch of regimental pattern ; and the 8th and 17th Cavalry, light dragoon pouch with silver flap
**Pouch Belt** —Double gold or silver lace, 2½ inches wide with silk stripe up centre ; morocco lining and edging the colour of the facings (18th Lancers —Blue) ; silver plate, pickers (15th Lancers—Regimental crest, instead of prickers) and chains of regimental pattern   11th Lancers, pouch belt of regimental pattern
**Spurs.**—The 17th Cavalry wear straight necked spurs in levée dress
**Sword and Scabbard** —As in Appendix VIII   The 11th Lancers ; full dress sword and scabbard of regimental pattern.
**Sword Belt and Slings** —White silk web 2 inches wide, with 2 gilt or plated rings for slings   Slings of gold or silver and silk lace 1¼ inches wide ; fastened with buckle and leather straps   Morocco lining edging and silk stripe the colour of the facings (18th Lancers—Blue)
In review order with the kurta a sword belt two inches wide of double gold or silver lace with a silk stripe up the centre, and morocco lining and edging the colour of the facings, fastening in front with regimental pattern plate the same width as the belt
**Trousers** —Blue cloth with two cloth stripes of the colour of the facings, ¾ inch wide and ¼ inch apart, down the side seams   The 4th Cavalry and the 7th Lancers, scarlet, and the 1st Lancers and 16th Cavalry, yellow stripes

**Tunic** *(Optional)* —Cloth the colour of the uniform, double breasted, with lapels, sewn down, collars and cuffs of regimental facings (Plastron ; 1st Lancers, black ; 13th Lancers, scarlet)   Collar edged round the top with ¾ inch lace and with cord on the lower seam   Cuffs pointed and ornamented with a row of lace round the top   Two rows of buttons in front, 7 in each row, the bottom one flat to go under the girdle ; rows 8 inches apart at the top and 4 inches at the waist ; 2 buttons at the waist behind and 2 small buttons on the sleeves   Blue slash on each skirt, edged with square cord, three buttons on each flap   A welt of the regimental facings (16th Cavalry, yellow) in the sleeve and back seams, down the front and round the skirts   Skirts lined with black   Gold or silver wire shoulder cords lined with cloth the colour of the tunic, small button at the top ; badges of rank in gold or silver embroidery according to lace

*Undress*

119   **Frock** —As in para 25, but with piping of the colour of the regimental facings in the sleeve, down the back seams and round the collar and cuffs   In the 16th Cavalry the piping is yellow   The 1st Lancers wear a blue serge frock with yellow piping

**Gloves** —As in para 26

Other articles as in Full Dress   Pouch belt not worn

*Mess Dress*

120   **Mess Jacket**:—As in para 107 but with piping of regimental facings (16th Cavalry—yellow) in the sleeve and down the back seams   Dummies at back seams   Two small buttons on each cuff   The 13th Lancers wear the tunic shoulder cords with the mess jacket

*Horse Furniture*

121   **Throat Ornaments** —

|             |   |   |           |
|-------------|---|---|-----------|
| 1st Lancers | . |   | Black.    |
| 2nd Lancers | . |   | Scarlet.  |
| 10th Lancers| . | . | Scarlet   |
| 17th Cavalry| . |   | White     |

**38th AND 39th CENTRAL INDIA HORSE.**

## British Officers.

*Full Dress.*

122   **Kurta**—Regimental pattern

**Lace** —Gold, light Dragoon pattern

**Pantaloons** —White doe skin

**Pouch.**—Silver, 7¼ inches × 2¾ inches, red box ; gilt badges on flap ; Prince of Wales' plume in silver

**Pouch Belt** —Two stripes of gold ⅞ inch lace, maroon velvet in centre, made up on white morocco with edging of maroon velvet   Gilt wave buckle, tip and slide

**Sword Belt** —Two stripes of lace ¾ inch wide showing ¼ inch maroon velvet in centre ; lined with maroon leather ; or a web belt as described in Appendix II(b)

**Slings** ½ inch lace showing ⅛ inch maroon velvet in centre ; gilt oval buckles

**Sword Knot** —Gold line with acorn

**Trousers** —Cloth drab double stripe the colour of the facings, showing ¼ inch piping of drab between

**Tunic** *(Optional)* —Cloth, drab, with maroon velvet collar and cuffs, braided with round back gold cord   Single breasted lined throughout with drab silk and edged all round with gold round back cord   Gold round back cord on the back seams forming three eyes at the top passing under a netted cap button at the waist, below which it is doubled, and terminating in an Austrian knot ¾ inch from the bottom of the skirt   Waist long   Collar cut square ; laced round the top with ¾ inch gold lace and edged all round the top and bottom with round back cord ; a row of heavy Russia braid along the bottom   Breast knots five drop loops, of gold round-back cord, with single eyes in centre   Gold netted caps in the drops, fastening with 5 gold olivets   Sleeves trimmed gold   Austrian knot of gold round back cord traced inside and out gold Russia braid   Shoulder straps

Hussar pattern, plaited gold chain gimp lined with drab, fastened by regimental pattern button   Badges of rank in silver embroidery

*Undress*

123  **Breeches** —Bedford cord
**Frock** —Drab serge, as in para 25
**Gloves** —Brown leather
Other articles as in Full Dress   Pouch belt not worn

*Mess Dress*

124  **Mess Jacket** —Drab cloth, with maroon velvet stand up collar and cuffs. Cuffs laced gold   Gold gimp chain on collar seam ; gold barrels at back. Shoulder straps as for tunic.   Gilt studs down left front, to fasten with hooks and eyes
**Trousers and Spurs** —As in Full Dress

*Hot Weather Uniform when on duty with the men*

125  **Hungarian Jacket** —Khaki drill, regimental pattern, with shoulder chains and badges of rank and regimental numerals
**Pantaloons.**—Light Bedford cord.
**Trousers** —Khaki drill with foot chains

**29th AND 30th LANCERS**

**British Officers**

*Full Dress*

126  **Cap Lines.**—Gold gimp and orris cord, with slide and olive ends passing round the body and looped on the left breast.
**Gauntlets.**—White doeskin with enamelled leather gauntlets
**Girdle** —Gold lace, $2\frac{1}{2}$ inches wide, with two white silk stripes ; lined dark green morocco leather
**Helmet** —As in para 29   *30th Lancers*—Bound in leather, hog spear spike on a bright leaf base.
**Kamarband.**—Kashmir shawl of regimental pattern
**Kurta.**—*29th Lancers*—Serge, dark green, opening down the front sufficiently to admit the head, pleat in front, 2 inches wide, fastened with 3 small gilt half ball buttons ; stand up collar $1\frac{1}{4}$ inches high, cut square in front, fastened with two hooks and eyes ; edged round the top with $\frac{3}{4}$ inch gold lace ; plain sleeves not exceeding 6 inches in width at the wrist and edged with inch lace   Two outside breast pockets with 3 pointed flaps and small gilt half ball button   Steel shoulder chains of regimental pattern.  *30th Lancers*—Serge, dark green, opening down the whole of the front, fastened with four small gilt half ball buttons, stand up white melton collar, 2 inches high, cut square in front, fastened with two hooks and eyes, edged round top and fronts with $\frac{3}{4}$ inch gold lace ; cuffs similar to mess jacket, pointed white melton cloth, $\frac{3}{4}$ inch gold lace edging, no pockets, steel shoulder chains of regimental pattern
**Lace** —Gold, Lancer pattern
**Pantaloons** —With the kurta, white melton cloth   On other occasions, rifle green cloth with stripes as for trousers
**Pouch** —Dark green morocco leather, solid metal bright gilt flap, $6\frac{1}{2}$ inches long and $2\frac{3}{4}$ inches deep, with chased $\frac{1}{8}$ inch border ; regimental device in gilt
**Pouch Belt** —Gold lace to match girdle, 2 inches wide with $\frac{1}{4}$ inch full white stripe down the centre   Dark green morocco leather lining and edging ; silver engraved buckle  tip and slide, with prickers and chains ; plate of regimental pattern
**Sword Belt and Slings** —White web, 2 inches wide, with snake fastening ; dees for sword slings ; slings of gold lace $1\frac{1}{4}$ inch wide with $\frac{1}{8}$ inch white silk stripe down the centre, dark green morocco leather lining and edging  round gilt buckles and leather straps
**Sword Knot.** –Gold cord and acorn
**Trousers.**—Cloth, rifle green, with two stripes the colour of the facings, $\frac{3}{4}$ inch wide and $\frac{1}{4}$ inch apart down the side seams

**Tunic.**—(*Optional*) Cloth, rifle green double breasted, (29th Lancers - Plastron 30th Lancers—Lapel), collar, cuffs, plastron or lapel of regimental facings Cuffs pointed with one row of one inch lace; two small buttons at the cuffs Collar edged round the top with ¾ inch lace and with gold wire square cord on the lower seam   Two rows of buttons in front, 7 in each row, bottom one flat to go under girdle; rows 8 inches apart at the top and 4 inches at the bottom; two buttons at the waist behind   A slash on each back skirt edged with gold wire square cord, 3 buttons on each flap   A welt of regimental facings in the sleeve and back seams, down the front and round the skirts which are lined with black silk   Shoulder straps of gold wire cord lined with white, small button at the top; badges of rank in silver embroidery

### Undress

127  **Frock**—As in para  25, but with piping of the colour of the regimental facings in the sleeve, down the back seams and round the collar and cuffs
**Gloves**—As in para. 26
Other articles as in Full Dress   Pouch belt not worn

### Mess Dress

128  **Mess Jacket**—Cloth, rifle green, as in para  107, but with a welt of regimental facings up the sleeves and down the back seams   Two small buttons on each cuff   Lining white twilled silk
**Trousers and Spurs**—As in Full Dress

#### 26th, 27th AND 28th LIGHT CAVALRY

### British Officers.

#### Full Dress

129  **Cap Lines**—Gold gimp and orris cord, with slide and olive ends
**Girdle**—Gold lace, 2½ inches wide, with two crimson silk stripes
**Helmet.**—As in para  29   Fittings, silver
**Lace**—Silver vandyke pattern
**Pouch**—Red morocco leather, with silver embroidered edging, round top, solid silver flap, 7½ inches wide and 2¾ inches deep, engraved round the edges, silver staples
**Pouch Belt**—Silver lace, 2½ inches wide, ¼ inch silk line in centre morocco leather lining and edging as for sword belt   Silver engraved plate, chains and prickers   Silver ornamented buckle, tip and slide, regimental badge in frosted silver
**Scabbard**—Steel, with horse shoe bottom and trumpet shaped mouth
**Sword Belt and Slings**—Web—As in Appx  11(b)   Slings of silver and silk lace 1¼ inches wide; silk lines, morocco edging and lining of the colour of the facings
**Sword Knot**—Gold and crimson cord with gold acorn
**Trousers and Pantaloons**—Sky blue with two stripes of the colour of the facings ¾ inch wide and ¼ inch apart, down the side seams
**Tunic**—French grey, as in para 118; skirts lined with drab  Shoulder straps of silver wire cord lined with buff, badges of rank in gold embroidery

#### Undress

130  **Frock**—As in para 25, but with piping the colour of the facings in the sleeves, down the back seams, and round the collar and cuffs
**Gloves**—As in para  26
Other articles as in Full Dress   Pouch belt not worn

#### Mess Dress

131  **Mess Jacket**—French grey, as in  para  120, with silver studs down the front and silver chain gimp round bottom of collar
**Trousers and Spurs**—As in Full Dress

31st, 32nd AND 37th LANCERS

## British Officers

*Full Dress*

**132  Cap Lines** —Gold gimp and orris cord with slide and olive ends

**Gauntlets.**—31st and 32nd, white buckskin ; 37th, brown leather

**Girdle** —Gold lace 2½ inches wide, with 2 crimson silk stripes

**Kamarband** —Regimental pattern

**Kurta** —Cloth or serge piped down the seams of the sleeves and back with piping the colour of the facings

**Lace** —Gold zig zag pattern    (37th Lancers—Gold, Dragoon pattern )

**Pantaloons.**—With the kurta  31st and 32nd Lancers—White moleskin 37th Lancers—Bedford cord   On other occasions—Blue diagonal cloth with stripes as for trousers.

**Pouch** —Silver, 7½ inches by 2¾ inches ; silver buckle ; lined red morocco.

**Pouch Belt** —Two and a quarter inches wide of double gold lace ⅞ inch wide ; ¼ inch  red silk stripe, lined morocco ; buckles, tip, slides, whistle and chain, plain silver, regimental pattern

**Sword Belt** —Red web, with slings of gold lace, 1¼ inches wide ⅛ inch silk stripe in the centre

**Sword Knot.**—Gold and red cord, with gold acorn

**Trousers.**—Cloth, dark blue, with two stripes of  the colour of  the facings, ¾ inch wide and ¼ inch apart, down the side seams

**Tunic** —(*32nd Lancers*)—Cloth, dark blue double, breasted, with plastron, collar and cuffs of regimental facings ; cuffs 5¼ inches deep at the point,  1¼ inch at back seam   Collar and cuffs ornamented with one inch lace round  the top   Two rows of buttons in front, 7 in each row, the bottom ones flat;  rows 8 inches apart at the top and 4 inches at the bottom, 2 buttons at the waist behind   A flap on each skirt at the back, edged with square gold cord, 3 buttons on each flap   A piping of regimental facings in  the sleeves and back seams, down the front and round  the skirts  which are lined with white   Gold wire shoulder cords   Badges of rank in silver embroidery

*Undress*

**133  Frock** —As in para  25  with piping  the colour of the facings  up  the sleeves down the back seams and round the collar and cuffs

**Gloves** —As in para  26.

Other articles as in Full Dress   Pouch belt not worn

*Mess Dress*

**134**  Blue as in para  116, but with piping  of the colour of the facings on back seams and sleeves of the jacket

*Horse Furniture*

**135  Throat Ornaments** –

| | |
|---|---|
| 31st  Lancers | Scarlet |
| 32nd  Lancers | White |
| 37th  Lancers | Scarlet |

20th DECCAN HORSE

## British Officers

*Full Dress*

**136.  Gauntlets** —White doe skin with white enamalled leather gauntlets

**Helmet.**—As in para  29, with hog spear spike on a bright leaf base

**Kamarband** —Kashmir shawl.   Regimental pattern

**Kurta** — Cloth, rifle  green   White collar ; ¾ inch Hussar lace round collar, down front to waist, and round cuffs   Gimp lace round bottom of collar   Shoulder chains on white cloth

**Lace** — Gold Hussar pattern

**Lungi** —Blue

**Pantaloons** —White melton cloth.

**Pouch** —Dark green morocco leather, solid metal bright gilt flap, $6\frac{1}{2}$ inches long, $2\frac{3}{4}$ inches deep, chased $\frac{1}{2}$ inch border, regimental device in silver

**Pouch Belt** —Gold Hussar lace 2 inches wide with $\frac{1}{4}$ inch full white silk stripe down the centre   Dark green morocco leather lining and edging   Silver engraved buckle tip and slide with prickers and chains, plate of regimental pattern.

**Sword Belt and Slings** —Lace as for pouch belt; buckle with regimental badge

**Sword Knot** —Gold cord and acorn

**Trousers** — Cloth, rifle green, with a stripe of $1\frac{1}{2}$ inch white melton cloth down the side seams

*Undress*

137  **Frock** —As in para  25

**Gloves** —As in para  26

**Pantaloons** —Cloth, rifle green ; stripes as for trousers

Other articles as in Full Dress   Pouch belt not worn

*Mess Dress*

138  **Mess Jacket** —Cloth, rifle green long waisted, pointed behind and cut out over the hips, studs down the front   Collar and pointed cuffs of facing cloth   Lining white twilled silk   Shoulder straps of plain cloth of the colour of the jacket and edged with $\frac{1}{2}$ inch lace   Badges of rank in gold embroidery   Lace $\frac{1}{2}$ inch wide

**Trousers and Spurs** —As in Full Dress

*Horse  Furniture*

139  **Throat Ornament** —Red

ADEN TROOP

### British Officers

140  Full Dress, when not parading with the troop, that of the corps to which they permanently belong   When parading with the men, khaki drill

INDIAN OFFICERS

3rd SKINNERS, 9th HODSON'S HORSE, 4th. 5th, 6th, 8th, 12th, 16th and  17th  CAVALRY, 1st  2nd, 7th, 10th  11th  13th, 14th, 15th  18th and 19th LANCERS

*Full Dress*

141  **Boots, Girdle, Kurta, Kamarband, Lungi,  Pantaloons  Sword** — Regimental pattern

**Lace, Pouch, Pouch Belt, Spurs, Sword Belt** —As for British officers

**Pyjamas** —White or " Multani ' colour as worn by the men

**Horse Furniture** —Regimental pattern

**H  W  Uniform** —Regimental Pattern.

The 11th Lancers wear the Prince of Wales  plume on  the shoulder chains instead of the  regimental numerals

*Undress*

142  **Cloak and Cape, Kamarband,  Kurta, Lungi,  Pantaloons and Pyjamas** —Regimental pattern

Other articles as in Full Dress   Pouch belt not worn

*Service Dress*

143  Regimental pattern

**21st, 22nd 23rd AND 25th CAVALRY**

*Full Dress*

144  **Boots** —Regimental pattern
**Kamai band** —Kashmir, or gold embroidered shawl of regimental pattern
**Kurta** —Regimental colour, loose, with or without collar, open to the waist
and fastened with round buttons    The skirt to reach to within 3 inches of the
knee, cuffs of regimental facings similar to that of British officers; edging of ¾
inch lace round neck, breast and cuffs; metal shoulder chains (*25th Cavalry*—
Twisted gold cord )    Badges of rank in white metal
**Lungi** —Regimental pattern
**Pyjamas** —White; 25th Cavalry—Grey fustian
**Pouch, Pouch Belt, Spurs, Sword Belt** —As for British officers in Full
Dress
**Sword and Scabbard** —Regimental pattern
**H W Uniform** —Regimental pattern

*Undress*

145  **Boots** —Ankle, with putties
**Great coat, Kamarband, Kurta, Lungi** —Regimental pattern
**Horse Furniture** —Regimental  pattern
Other articles as in Full Dress    Pouch belt not worn

*Service Dress*

146  Regimental pattern

**31st, 32nd, 37th LANCERS ; ADEN TROOP ; 33rd, 34th, 35th AND 36th HORSE**
147  Uniform to conform as far as possible to that of British officers
The Aden Troop wear khaki drill
**Horse Furniture** —Regimental pattern    Throat ornament as for British
officers    Aden Troop —Throat ornament, white
**Kurta** —Collar and cuffs of regimental  facings, trimmed with 1 inch lace
Badges of  rank in silver metal    In Lancer regiments the kurta is piped down
the seams
**Scabbard** —Steel or white metal for review order, brown leather for other
duties
**Sword** —Curved tulwar

**38th AND 39th CENTRAL INDIA HORSE**

*Full Dress*

148  **Belts** —As for British officers ; frog in place of slings
**Boots** —Regimental pattern
**Great coat** —Regimental pattern
**Kamai band** —Scarlet, Kashmir  work
**Kurta** —Serge, drab, with gold tracing braid round collar, down front and
on sleeves, ¾ inch regimental pattern ; buttons down front ; nickel plated steel
shoulder chains with silver badges of rank
**Lungi** —Blue ends striped with white and shades of blue
**Pyjamas.—**White
**Scabbard** —Brown leather, brass tip
**Spurs.—**As for British officers
**Sword** —Half basket hilt, black fishskin grip bound with silver wire ;  curved
blade 32 inches long and 1½ inches wide at the shoulder, grooved and spear
pointed
**Horse Furniture** —Regimental pattern
**H W Uniform** —Khaki kurta, yellow pyjamas, blue and white cotton lungi
red kamarband, boots and putties

*Undress*

149  As in Full Dress but with Sam Browne belts ; khaki pyjamas

*Service Dress.*

150  Regimental pattern

## 20th DECCAN HORSE 29th AND 30th LANCERS

### Full Dress

**151  Belt, Gauntlets, Pouch, and Spurs** —As for British officers
**Boots, Great coat, Lungi, Scabbard, and Sword** —Regimental pattern
**Kamarband** —*20th Deccan Horse* —Red shawl, green border ; *29th and 30th Lancers*—Red shawl, regimental pattern
**Kurta** —Cloth, rifle green, loose, open to waist and fastened with 3 small round gilt buttons ; gold lace ¾ inch wide round neck, breast and cuffs  Skirts to reach to within 3 inches of the knee  Steel shoulder chains, badges of rank in silver
**Horse Furniture** —Regimental pattern
**H W Uniform**—Regimental pattern

### Undress

**152  Belt** —Sam Browne
**Boots** —Regimental pattern
**Kurta** —Khaki drill
**Lungi** —Regimental pattern
**Pantaloons** —Khaki
**Spurs** —As for British officers    Pouch belt not worn

### Service Dress

**153**  Regimental pattern

## 26th, 27th and 28th LIGHT CAVALRY

### Full Dress

**154  Boots** —Mounted —Regimental pattern
Dismounted —Ankle
**Great coat, Horse Furniture and Kamarband** —Regimental pattern
**Kurta** —Serge, Cavalry grey, (Indian officers' quality) open down the front ; from collar seam down to 14 inch the front is traced with three rows of silver braid on the edge ⅜ inch apart and three rows ½ inch apart 2½ inch from edge ; between the rows of braid are the button holes and buttons, the buttons are of German Silver—Large G R I  From 14 inches down, the right skirt is cut 6 inches wider so as to pass well under the left skirt when fastened  The back is opened at 17½ inch down from collar seam  Shoulder chains fastened on to a piece of the body material by five hooks  Two outside breast pockets on each side, with a loose pleat behind, depth at front from top of flap 6¼ inches, at back 7 inches, width 6½ inches, the flaps are pointed at the centre, depth from top of flap to point 3½ inches with hole and button  Collar of the same material as body cloth 1½ inch deep cut square at front fastened with two hooks and eyes  silver lace ⅛ inch round the top and down the front, traced on either side by silver braid which is also carried along the bottom  Cuffs pointed with ⅛ inch silver lace carried right round, the point of the silver lace being 7 inches from the bottom of cuff at centre and 2½ inches at sides  the lace is traced on both sides by silver braid forming a flowered knot over the point, and a crow s foot pointing downwards underneath
**Lungi** —Regimental pattern
**Pantaloons** —Cloth, sky blue, superfine, cut as for British cavalry with two ¾ inch buff pale superfine stripes down each side seam, ¼ inch of body material showing between the 2 stripes, full knee, seat strapping and sword patch ' V ' let in at waist on underside  Small fob pocket on right top side
**Scabbard** —Wood covered with black leather ; steel mountings
**Spurs** —As for British officers
**Sword** —Tulwar, scroll hilt, blade 32 inches long
**Sword Belt** —Brown leather with braces
**Sword Knot** —Brown leather

### Service Dress

**155**  Regimental pattern

CORPS OF GUIDES —CAVALRY AND INFANTRY

## British Officers

*Full Dress*

156  **Boots** —Mounted —Black butcher
          Dismounted —Brown ankle.
**Gloves** —White buckskin
**Great coat.**—As in para 28 or regimental pattern
**Helmet** —As in para 29   Silver fittings
**Lace.**—Drab silk
**Pouch** —Brown bridle leather, with silver flap cover, with regimental device.
**Pouch Belt** —Plain brown leather edged with silver   chain, buckle, tip and slide of regimental pattern, with chain and prickers
**Scabbard** —Regimental pattern
**Spurs** —As in para 40
**Sword** —As in Appendix VIII
**Sword Belt and Slings** —Brown leather, regimental pattern
**Sword Knot** —Brown and silver strap, with acorn
**Trousers and Pantaloons** —Cloth, drab, with a double stripe of drab lace $\frac{3}{4}$ inch wide, with a welt the colour of the facings between the stripes
**Tunic** —Cloth, drab, Hussar pattern, with collar and cuffs of regimental facings; edged all round, except collar, with drab silk cord; collar laced round the top with $\frac{3}{4}$ inch drab silk lace, and on the seam with one row of heavy Russia braid ; five quadruple rows of drab silk cord  hanging loose across the breast   Sleeves laced ; an Austrian knot of drab silk square cord reaching to 8 inches from the bottom of the cuff and  traced  with braid ; shoulder  straps   of plaited drab silk lined with drab and with a small button at the top, badges of rank in silver embroidery

*Undress*

157  **Forage Cap.**—As in para  19 with scarlet band and welts
**Frock** —As in para 25 but with cuffs of red velvet ; silver buttons.
**Gloves** —As in para 26.
**Pantaloons** —Drab cord
Other articles as in Full Dress   Pouch belt not worn

*Mess Dress*

158. **Mess Jacket** —As in para  111 but with shoulder straps of plaited drab silk and badges of rank in silver embroidery   No studs down the front

**Mess Waistcoat** —Scarlet, fastened up to throat, with gold braid  and gilt studs down the front; gold braid along the pockets

**Trousers and Spurs** —As in Full Dress

*Hot Weather Uniform and Service Dress.*

159  Universal pattern   See General Instructions
The mess jacket has a red piping round the jacket, collar and cuffs

*Horse Furniture*

160  **Universal Pattern** —Brow band, brown leather ; rosettes, silver

## Indian Officers

161   As in paras 144 and 145, with following exceptions :—

**Blouse** —(Infantry only) As in para 195

**Breeches.**—Cavalry, drab cord ; Infantry, khaki drill knickeibockeis

**Pouch** —Brown bridle leather with regimental device.

**Pouch Belt** —Brown biidle leather, buckle tip, slide, chains and prickers of regimental pattern

**Sword Belt and Slings** —Brown leather, regimental pattern

## PART VII
### INDIAN OFFICERS —MOUNTAIN ARTILLERY

162   **Belt.**—Sam Browne

**Boots** —Brown, ankle, as for British officers

**Cloak and Cape** —Regimental pattern

**Jacket** —Tartan, blue No 2, cut tunic shape, with waist seam ; fastened down the front with four large buttons, and one hook and eye at waist seam, two large buttons on waist seam at back   Two waist hooks, one on either side   The back is made with a yoke extending about 4 inches down from the collar seam The lower part of the back is provided with two pleats which are left loose for expansion   Pockets —An outside breast pocket with 1 inch box pleat down the centre and flap pointed at centre and slightly rounded at ends on each breast   The top of the flap being in line with the second button hole   The depth of the pocket from top of flap about 7 inches, width 6 inches.  Collar —Scarlet cloth 1½ inches in depth, slightly rounded at front,   fastened with one hook and eye.  Lace gold ¼ inch round the top and along the end   Gold braid No 3 along the bottom Gilding metal grenades   Shoulder Straps —Body cloth with gold braid No 3 all round, except at base, fastened with one small button at the neck ; badges of rank   Sleeves —No cuffs, but an Austrian knot of gold braid No 3.  The top of the knot being 8 inches from bottom of sleeve   The braid is not carried round to under half of sleeve but is finished off on top with an eye 1 inch from the bottom The front, skirt, collar and yoke are lined with black Italian cloth.

**Pagri** —Red, same shade as the regimental facings, 8 yards long and 1 yard wide

**Pantaloons** —Tartan, blue No 2 with scarlet cloth stripes 2 inches wide down the side seams   Seat and knee strappings of black moleskin   Small fob pocket on right top side

**Putties** —Blue, woollen

**Saddlery** —As laid down in Army Tables for Mountain Artillery

**Spurs.**—As for British officers

**Sword and Scabbard** —Regimental pattern

**Sword Knot.**—Brown leather

*Service Dress*

163.  **Jacket** —As for British officers, except that the collar will be stand up, cut square in front and fastened with 2 hooks and eyes   Five small buttons down the front.  Badges of rank—Silver ; letters of battery—Brass

**Lungi.**—Khaki, eight yards long, one yard wide with gold fringe 3 inches deep.

**Pantaloons.**—Khaki cord

**Putties** —Khaki

### INDIAN OFFICERS—FRONTIER GARRISON ARTILLERY

164   Uniform, etc   as above with the following exceptions :—

**Belt** —Waist, brown, with brown leather slings 1 inch wide   Gilt billet studs, oval wire buckles.

**Shoes.**—(Instead of boots) —Ordinary, country, brown

**Sword and Scabbard** —As for warrant officers

**Sword Knot.**—Brown, leather, with plaited acorn

*Service Dress*

165   **Knickerbockers.**—As for the men

## PART VIII

### SAPPERS AND MINERS

### BRITISH OFFICERS

166  As described for Royal Engineers in Dress Regulations for the Army

### INDIAN OFFICERS

167  **Boots** —Ankle

**Forage Cap** —No 15 (*Burma*) *Co  only*—Regimental pattern

**Great coat.**—Regimental pattern

**H W. Uniform and Service Dress** —Regimental pattern

**Pagri** —Regimental pattern

**Pouch.**—*1st S & M*  Brown leather—(To hold binoculars)  *2nd S  &  M* Brown leather gilt mountings  *3rd S  &  M* —Black patent leather, as for British officers

**Pouch Belt and Sword Belt.**—Brown leather with gilt mountings  *2nd S & M* —Pouch belt brown leather  2½ inches wide

**Putties** —Dark blue

**Pyjamas.**—(*3rd S  & M* —Knicker bockers)  Blue serge, with scarlet stripes 1⅞ inches wide down the side seams

**Sword and Scabbard** —As laid down in Army Tables of Engineer Units

**Sword Knot** —Brown leather, as for British officers

**Trousers** —*2nd S & M* Blue serge with scarlet cloth stripes  2 inches wide down the side seams

**Tunic**—*1st S & M* —Scarlet cloth, collar and cuffs garter blue cloth The collar edged round the front and top with ½ inch gold lace, and round the bottom with round back  gold cord   Cuffs pointed and ornamented with an Austrian knot of round back gold cord extending to 8 inches from bottom of cuff ; 5 buttons in front ; front and skirt edged with garter blue cloth   Skirt rounded off in front and lined with white   Shoulder knots of round-back gold cord, R E pattern, lined with scarlet, small button at the top   Badges of rank in silver embroidery

*2nd S & M* —Scarlet cloth, with  collar and cuffs of plush blue worsted; collar 1¾ inches high rounded off in front and edged with narrow gold cord along the top and bottom ; cuffs 1¾ inches deep, with peak in front 2¾ inches high, gold cord along the top forming an Austrian knot above the peak extending to 7½ inches from bottom of cuff ; 9 buttons in front and 2 at the waist behind ; skirt rounded off in front and closed behind with a pleat at each side and lined with white shalloon ; body back and sleeves lined with white cotton ; the left front skirts and pleats edged with blue worsted tape ; pocket inside left breast   Shoulder straps edged with ½ inch gold lace, and fastened with small button, badges of rank in silver embroidery

*3rd S & M* —As for British officers

*Nos 31 and 32 (Divisional Signal) Companies* —Uniform as for 1st S and M with the exception of badges and devices special to the Corps

*Nos 33 and 34 (Divisional Signal) Companies* —Uniform as for 2nd S and M with the exception of badges and devices special to the Corps

## PART IX

### INDIAN INFANTRY

### GENERAL

168  Unless otherwise stated the following articles are universal for all Indian Infantry Regiments :—

**Boots** —As in para  16
**Forage Cap** —As in para  19
**Frock Serge** —As in para  25
**Gloves** —As  in para  26
**Great coat.**—As in para  28
**Helmet.**—As in para  29.
**H  W  Uniform  and  Service  Dress** —Universal  pattern    See  General Instructions
**Horse Furniture** —As in para  58
**Pagri** —Regimental pattern
**Spurs.**—As in para  40
**Sword Belt** —Web, as in Appendix 11(*b*)

In regiments in which Indian  officers wear  the  blouse  and  kamarband  the latter need only be worn in review order

### REGIMENTS DRESSED IN SCARLET

## British Officers

### *Full Dress*

169  **Lace** —Gold, half inch  vellum pattern
**Pantaloons.**—Blue cloth, scarlet welt $\frac{1}{4}$ inch  wide  down the side seams.
**Pouch** —107th and  128th Pioneers —Binocular  case  of  brown  leather,  5 by 2 inches  top $3\frac{1}{2}$ by $1\frac{1}{4}$ inches  bottom 4 inches deep with brown leather  cover Badge as in Appendix I
**Pouch Belt** —107th and 128th Pioneers —Brown  leather, with $\frac{3}{4}$ inch  gilt chain on the edges and regimental badges as in Appendix I.
**Sash** —Crimson  silk, as in para 37    The 107th and 128th Pioneers wear no sash, but in its place, over the tunic a brown  leather belt and slings edged with $\frac{3}{8}$ inch  gold sewing and regimental badge on buckle
**Sword Knot** —Gold and crimson strap, with gold acorn
**Sword Slings** —Gold lace, British Infantry pattern, $\frac{7}{8}$ inch  wide, on red morocco leather 1 inch wide  gilt billet studs, on oval wire buckles
**Sword and  Scabbard** —As in  Appendix  VIII, with Royal and Imperial Cypher and Crown on hilt
**Trousers.**—Blue cloth, scarlet welt $\frac{1}{4}$ inch wide down the side seams
**Tunic** —Scarlet cloth with collar and cuffs of regimental facings    Collar rounded off in front and ornamented with $\frac{1}{2}$ inch lace  along  the  top, and  gold Russia at the bottom ;  badges  as  in Appendix I  Cuffs pointed, with $\frac{1}{2}$ inch lace round  the  top, extending to $7\frac{1}{2}$ inches, and a tracing in gold Russia braid $\frac{3}{16}$ inch above and below the lace, forming an Austrian knot at the top extending to $9\frac{1}{2}$ inches from the bottom of the cuff    Eight buttons in front    The skirt closed behind, edged with white cloth on closing seam with a 3 pointed  slash on each side, a button on each point   The front, collar  and  slashes edged with white cloth $\frac{1}{4}$ inch wide   Twisted round gold shoulder cords, universal pattern, lined with scarlet, a small button of regimental  pattern  at the top

### *Undress*

170  **Forage Cap** —As in para 19
**Frock** —As in para. 25
Other articles as in Full Dress—no sash or pouch belt

### *Mess Dress*

171.  **Mess Jacket** —Scarlet cloth or kerseymere ; collar, cuffs,  and  shoulder straps of cloth the colour of the facings (102nd Grenadiers—Red silk collar) ; collar rolled, cuffs pointed    Trimmed with  plain white piping round  the  edge,  collar, cuffs,  and  shoulder  straps ; scarlet lining ; shoulder straps  sewn  down  under

the collar; no studs or buttons on any part of the jacket; badges of rank in gilt or gilding metal

**Mess Waistcoat** —Cloth or kerseymere of the colour of the facings, except with white, buff or yellow facings in which cases the waistcoat may be scarlet ; cut plain and open in front, and fastened with 4 small gilt buttons of regimental pattern ; plain pocket on each side  A plain open white washing waistcoat, without lapels, and fastened by 4 small buttons as above may be adopted at the option of units but all officers of a unit to be dressed alike

**Trousers,**—As in Full Dress

*Horse Furniture*

172  **Universal Pattern** —Brow band and rosettes of the colour of the facings

## Indian Officers

173  **Blouse** —*(2nd, 10th, 48th, 66th, 95th 97th, 99th, and 109th Infantry)*— Serge, scarlet, ordinary, length 40 inches to fit a man 5 feet 9 inches to 5 feet 10 inches varying 1½ inches for every 2 inches in height.  Collar 1½ inches in depth of facing cloth, slightly rounded at front and fastened with one hook and eye with ⅛ inch gold lace round the ends and along the top ; lined with scarlet Italian cloth   Shoulder straps of facing cloth with ½ inch gold lace all round except at base, fastening at neck with two small buttons   Cuffs of facing cloth 6½ inches deep at front and 2¼ inches at side and back, ½ inch gold lace all round showing ⅛ inch of facing cloth  Opening in front 16½ inches in length made up 2¼ inches wide, edged on both sides with ¼ inch of facing cloth, fastened in centre with three large buttons with a small hook and eye at top to fix to collar seam   Opening at side seam at bottom 6 inches in length   Kamarbands for wear with the blouse are of the colour of the regimental facings

**Boots** —Regimental pattern

**Great coat and Cape.**— Regimental pattern

**H W Uniform and Service Dress** —Khaki, regimental pattern

**Kamarband** —Regimental pattern

**Knickerbockers** —Serge blue ordinary (quality optional)   The knicker bockers are cut loose, the spare material being fitted into a waist band 2¼ inches wide to give plenty of room over the hips   The waist band is lined cotton, grey, and fastened with a drawstring running through the centre   Fly fronted with three buttons  Piping of scarlet down side seam ¼ inch in width  The bottoms of the knickerbockers are made loose and provided with a drawstring for fastening below the knee, the string being covered as the knickerbockers are cut long enough to fall over about 4 inches

**Pagri** —Regimental pattern    Badges as in Appendix I

**Pouch and Pouch Belt.**—107th and 128th Pioneers  As for British officers.

**Sash** —As for British officers   The sash is not worn by Indian officers of the 2nd, 10th, 48th, 66th, 95th, 97th 99th and 109th Infantry.

**Scabbard.**—Steel   (44th, 94th and 99th Infantry—Brown leather, if provided regimentally )   In service dress as for British officers

**Sword** —As in Appendix VIII, with Royal and Imperial Cypher on the outer boss of the hilt

**Sword Belt** —Web, khaki, with brown leather slings   For regiments which do not wear the waist sash —Brown leather 2 inches wide with leather slings ; clasp, flap and gilt hook

**Sword Knot** —Brown leather, ½ inch wide, with acorn and brass buckle

**Tunic**—*(Except 2nd, 10th, 48th, 66th, 95th, 97th, 99th and 109th Infantry)*— Cloth scarlet No 1, with a piping of facing cloth ¼ inch wide down the left front and from bottom button to the bottom of tunic on the right front, also right centre of back skirt ; collar 1½ inches in depth, of facing cloth, slightly rounded at front and fastened with one hook and eye, with ½ inch gold lace round the ends and along the top; shoulder straps of facing cloth with ½ inch gold lace all round except at base ; cuffs of facing cloth pointed 6½ inches deep in front and 2¼ inches at side and back ½ inch gold lace all round showing ¼ inch of facing cloth ; eight large buttons down front, two at skirt behind, and two small buttons on shoulder straps   The sleeves and fronts are lined with white cotton; waist hook in seam on both sides　A pocket up and down inside left breast

**White Spats or Leggings**—May be worn in Full Dress when authorised, if provided regimentally

## REGIMENTS DRESSED IN GREEN

### British Officers

*Full Dress*

174　**Boots** —As in para 16.　*127th Baluch L I, 129th and 130th Baluchis* Mounted—Brown leather　Black leather when not parading with troops

**Braid** —Black mohair

**Gloves** —Black leather　(42nd Deoli, 43rd Erinpura, 127th Baluch L I, 129th and 130th Baluchis—Brown leather )

**Great coat** —As in para 28　The 42nd and 43rd may wear the Pea Jacket, khaki, as in para 34 instead of the universal pattern great-coat, but all officers of a unit must be dressed alike

**Helmet** —As in para 29　*55th Rifles, 127th Baluch L I, 129th and 130th Baluchis* —Silver fittings

**Lines** —Gurkha Regiments and 55th Rifles, as for British Rifle Regiments Hooked on the right breast 2 inches from the seam of the sleeve.

**Pouch** —Black patent leather (*55th, 104th, 123rd, and 125th*—Black leather; *127th, 129th, 130th*—Brown leather; *3rd, 7th, 9th, 39th*—Black enamelled seal leather) with badges as in Appx I.　The *5th Gurkhas* and *39th Garhwalis* wear a binocular case　*42nd Deoli and 43rd Erinpura Regiments* —Brown leather, with badge as in Appx I　Gilt chain edging in *43rd*

**Pouch Belt** —Black patent leather (*3rd, 7th, 9th Gurkhas and 39th Garhwalis*—Black enamelled seal leather; *127th, 129th, 130th*—Brown leather: black, when not parading with troops) 2⅜ inches wide (3 inches wide in *55th, 104th, 123rd, 125th Rifles; 127th, 129th and 130th Baluchis; 2nd and 5th Gurkhas*) with silver regimental plate, whistle and chain　*2nd Gurkhas*, bronze plate—As in Appx I　*42nd Deoli Regiment* brown leather with regimental device, whistle and chain in bronze；*43rd Erinpura Regiment* brown leather with gilt buckles, tip and slide；edging, whistle and chain in gilt

**Trousers and Pantaloons** —Rifle green cloth with 2 inch black braid down the side seams　*43rd Erinpura Regiment and 55th Rifles*, 2 stripes of mohair braid ⅞ inch wide on a scarlet ground with a light between the stripes　*127th Baluch L I, 129th and 130th Baluchis* —Red cloth plain　*42nd Deoli Regiment*—Scarlet cloth

*2nd Gurkha Rifles.*—As for King's Royal Rifle Corps

**Tunic** —Rifle green cloth, edged all round, except the collar, with black square cord　Black velvet collar and cuffs (*1st Gurkhas; 42nd Deoli and 43rd Erinpura Regiments; 104th, 123rd, 125th Rifles; 127th Baluch L I; 129th, and 130th Baluchis; 55th Coke's Rifles*—scarlet cloth)　Collar (rounded in front in case of the *42nd and 43rd, 55th 104th, 123rd, 125th, 127th, 129th, and 130th*) edged with ½ inch black braid with a tracing of plain braid below (the 42nd 43rd, and 55th have a black tracing of braid on the collar seam and the 5th Gurkhas have no tracing of braid below the edging of ½ inch braid); cuffs pointed in Austrian knot on the sleeve, with a tracing of plain braid round it, extending to 7 inches from the bottom of the cuff　The skirt rounded off in front, closed behind and lined with black　On each side of the breast 5 loops of black square cord, with netted caps and drops, fastening with black olivets　On each back seam a line of the same cord forming a crow's foot at the top, passing under a netted cap at the waist, below which it is doubled and ending in an Austrian knot reaching to the bottom of the skirt　Shoulder straps of black chain gimp rifle regiment pattern ; *42nd, 43rd 55th, 104th, 123rd, 125th, 127th 129th and 130th*—shoulder straps of Hussar pattern in black　Badges of rank in bronze (43rd gilt, 42nd and 55th showing a scarlet piping)　Collar badges as in Appx I

*2nd Gurkha Rifles* —As for King's Royal Rifle Corps

**Scabbard** —Steel

**Sword**—As in Appx VIII with device of bugle and crown on the hilt　(*42nd and 43rd*—As for Regiments dressed in Scarlet*)

**Sword, Belt and Slings.**—Web as in Appx 11(*b*)    Slings one inch wide black patent leather with square buckles (*3rd, 7th, 9th Gurkhas, 39th Garhwalis*—Black enamelled seal leather; *55th Rifles*—Black leather; *42nd Deoli Regiment and 43rd Erinpura Regiment*—Brown leather; *127th, Baluch L I, 129th,* and *130th Baluchis*—Brown leather: black when not parading with troops)

**Sword Knot** —Black leather (*42nd Deoli Regiment* and *43rd Erinpura Regiment*—Brown leather; *127th Baluch L I, 129th, 130th Baluchis*—Brown leather: black when not parading with troops) strap and acorn

*Undress*

175 **Forage Cap** —As in para 19
**Frock** —Green, as in para 25
Other articles as in Full Dress    Pouch belt not worn

*Mess Dress*

176 **Mess Jacket.**—Rifle green cloth, black velvet collar and cuffs (1st Gurkha Rifles scarlet facing cloth)    Black mohair braid all round the body, forming barrels (or dummies) at bottom of back seams   Back seams trimmed with a double row of ¼ inch mohair braid, forming a crow s foot at top and finishing over the barrels (or dummies) at the bottom   Pockets trimmed with ¼ inch mohair braid, forming a crow's foot at each end and in the centre   Five waved loops of square cord in front, with four rows of knitted olivets, two olivets on each loop   Pointed cuffs of inch mohair braid, with tracing of black Russia braid forming a row of small eyes on the outside and inside of the cuffs, and extending 6½ inches from the bottom of the cuff   Half inch mohair braid all round the collar trimmed through the centre with plumes, and a row of small eyes along top edge ; a loop at bottom of collar to fasten across the neck ; shoulder straps with badges of rank as on tunic
*1st Gurkha Rifles* —Scarlet facings
*2nd Gurkha Rifles* —As for King's Royal Rifle Corps
*5th Gurkha Rifles* —Rifle green cloth, black velvet collar and cuffs   Black mohair braid all round the body, forming barrels (or dummies) at bottom of back seams   Pockets trimmed with ¼ inch mohair braid, forming a crow's foot at each end and in the centre   Pointed cuffs of inch mohair braid, with tracing of black Russia braid forming a row of small eyes on the outside and inside of the cuffs, and extending 6½ inches from the bottom of the cuff   Half inch mohair braid all round the collar trimmed through the centre with plumes and a row of small eyes along top edge
*42nd Deoli and 43rd Erinpura Regts, 55th Coke s Rifles* —Rifle green cloth, hooks and eyes down the front, 4 loops on each side of breast, as on tunic, black mohair braid all round the body forming barrels (or dummies) at the bottom of back seams   Half inch braid all round the collar, with tracing braid all round inside forming an eye at each corner ; cuffs ornamented with inch mohair braid, 6 inches deep from bottom of cuff with tracing braid above and below, forming three eyes at the outer and one at the inner point ; shoulder straps as for tunic   Badges of rank in bronze (43rd, gilt)
*104th, 123rd 125th Rifles* —Rifle green cloth trimmed with inch mohair braid all round (except collar) barrels at bottom of side seams   Five wavy drop loops with single ends, two rows of olivets at both sides   Side seams braided with double ¼ inch braid forming crow's foot at top   Pockets trimmed with ¼ inch mohair braid forming three eyes in the centre, above and below, and crow s foot at both ends   Cuffs pointed with inch black mohair braid, figuring of black Russia braid above, and inside braid forming a crow's foot at point   Stand up collar trimmed with ½ inch braid all round with figuring inside   Shoulder cords and badges of rank as on tunic
*127th, Baluch L I and 129th 130th Baluchis* —Rifle green cloth with black studs and hooks and eyes down the front ; edged all round with black square cord ; collar and cuffs of regimental facings ; sleeve braided as for tunic   Black silk lining   Shoulder straps and badges of rank as for tunic
  **Mess Waistcoat** —Rifle green cloth no collar, open half way down, fastened with hooks and eyes   Half inch mohair braid on edges with ¼ inch braid down the front one inch from the edge   Pockets trimmed with ¼ inch mohair braid forming a crow s foot at each end

*1st Gurkha Rifles* —Scarlet cloth

*2nd Gurkhas* —As for King's Royal Rifle Corps

*5th Gurkhas* —Rifle green cloth fastened with hooks and eyes, edged with $\frac{1}{4}$ inch mohair braid and tracing of braid inside forming eyes at points; pockets with braid as for 55th Rifles

*42nd Deoli and 43rd Erinpura Regts and 55th Ooke's Rifles* —Scarlet cloth, hooked up to the throat No collar ; edged all round with black mohair tracing braid, and a row of eyes behind, forming a small Austrian knot at bottom of vest, two pockets edged with black tracing braid forming a crow's foot at each end and above and below the centre

*104th, 123rd, 125th Rifles* —Rifle green cloth, open half way down, trimmed with 2 lines of $\frac{1}{2}$ inch black mohair braid down the front, with $\frac{1}{4}$ inch scarlet cloth between with figuring of single eyes on top of the scarlet ; fastened with hooks and eyes ; pockets trimmed with $\frac{1}{4}$ inch braid underlaid with scarlet cloth, showing a narrow edge of scarlet on both sides of the braid, crow s foot at ends

*127th Baluch L I and 129th and 130th Baluchis* —Rifle green cloth, open half way down Hooks and eyes ; $\frac{1}{4}$ inch mohair braid on the edges with a second row of braid down the front, $\frac{3}{4}$ inch from the edge ; scarlet cloth between the two braids with a row of eyes of black Russia braid down front edge on the scarlet cloth Pockets trimmed with $\frac{1}{4}$ inch mohair braid forming a crow's foot at each end, edged all round with scarlet cloth

**Trousers** —As in Full Dress.

*2nd Gurkha Rifles* —As for King's Royal Rifle Corps

Hot weather mess dress (*Gurkha and Garhwal Regiments only*) —Thin dark green serge of the same pattern as the cloth mess dress No braid on jacket and with shoulder straps of the same material as the jacket

### Horse Furniture

177 **Universal Pattern** —Brown or black bridle. Brow band and rosettes green (*1st G R* green and scarlet rosettes) *127th Baluch L I and 129th and 130th Baluchis* —Brow band and rosettes brown

**Throat Ornament** —*1st Gurkhas ; 55th, 104th, 123rd, and 125th Rifles* — Black and scarlet horse hair, 18 inches long (*3rd, 4th, 5th, 6th, 7th, 8th, 9th, 10th Gurkhas, 39th Garhwalis*—Black horse hair), with silver ball and socket

**Shabraque** —*5th Gurkha Rifles* —Black astrakhan, edged with black cloth, scalloped, fastened by a leather surcingle

*2nd Gurkha Rifles* —As for King's Royal Rifle Corps

## Indian Officers

178 **Boots** —Regimental pattern

**Forage Cap** —(*Gurkha and Garhwal Rifles*) —Kilmarnock The 2nd Gurkha Rifles wear a diced border Badges as in Appx I

**Great coat and Cape.** —Regimental pattern.

**H W. Uniform and Service Dress** —Khaki, regimental pattern

**Knickerbockers** (*except Gurkha and Garhwal Rifles*) —Serge, green ordinary (optional, serge of Indian officers' quality) Cut loose with the looseness fitted into a waistband $2\frac{1}{4}$ inches wide to give plenty of room over the hips Waist band is lined with cotton, grey, and fastened with a drawstring running through the centre Fly fronted with three buttons Bottoms loose and provided with a drawstring for fastening below the knee, the string being covered as the knicker bockers are cut long enough to fall over about 4 inches

**Pagri** —Regimental pattern

**Pouch, Pouch Belt, Sword Belt, and Knot** —As for British officers Sword belts, black patent or brown leather $1\frac{1}{2}$ inches wide with slings 1 inch wide, german silver snake clasp and mountings may be worn in regiments for which they are authorised

**Scabbard** —Steel

**Sword** —As in Appx VIII

**Tunic** (*except 55th Rifles and Gurkha and Garhwal battalions*) —Cloth green, superfine, with a piping of facing cloth $\frac{1}{4}$ inch wide down the left front and from the bottom button to the bottom of tunic on the right front, also down centre of back skirt     Collar 1½ inches in depth made of facing cloth, rounded at front and fastened with one hook and eye, with ½ inch black silk lace round the ends and along the top     Shoulder straps  of facing cloth with ½ inch black silk lace all round except at base     Cuffs of facing cloth, pointed 6½ inches deep in front and 2¼ inches at side and back, ½ inch black silk lace all round showing ⅛ inch of facing cloth     Eight large buttons down front, two at skirt behind, and two small buttons for shoulder straps     The sleeves and fronts are lined with white cotton; waist hook in seam on both sides     A pocket up and down inside left breast

*Gurkha and Garhwal Rifle Regiments, with black facings* —Cloth  green superfine, with a piping of facing cloth ¼ inch wide down left front, skirt, pleats, and centre of back, and from bottom button to the bottom of tunic on the right front     Collar 1½ inches in depth made of facing cloth, slightly rounded at front and fastened with one hook and eye with ½ inch black silk lace all round     Shoulder straps made of body cloth, plain     Cuffs of facing cloth pointed 5½ inches deep in front, ½ inch black silk lace all round     The cuffs are rounded off at hind arm seam and the lace carried down each side of seam, finishing off  inside cuff     Eight large horn buttons, Rifle pattern down front, two at skirt behind, and two small horn buttons, Rifle pattern for shoulder straps     The sleeves and fronts are lined with white cotton ; waist hook in seam on both sides     A pocket up and down inside left breast

*Gurkha Rifle Regiments, with scarlet facings*

*1st Gurkha Rifles* —Instead of tunic the patrol jacket as for King's Royal Rifle Corps

*2nd Gurkha Rifles* —As for British Officers

**Trousers** (*Gurkha and Garhwal Rifles*) —Serge green, dark, Indian Officers, fly fronted, one small fob pocket on right side, side seam plain

*2nd Gurkha Rifles* —As for British Officers

### 104th, 123rd, AND 125th RIFLES

179  As above, with following exception :—

**Leggings** —Black canvas, with buckles and studs

### 127th BALUCH LIGHT INFANTRY ; 129th AND 130th BALUCHIS

180  As above, with following exceptions :—

**Knickerbockers** —Serge, red, ordinary ; regimental pattern (peg tops)
**Leggings** —White canvas with cord loops
**Tunic**—*129th Baluchis* —As for British officers, except that ¼ inch black braid takes the place of black square cord, and shoulder straps of the same cloth as the tunic are edged with ¼ inch black braid

### 55th COKE'S RIFLES

181  As above with following exception :—

**Tunic** —Cloth, green, superfine with a piping of facing cloth ¼ inch wide down the left front and from the bottom button to the bottom of tunic on the right front, also down centre of back skirt     Collar 1½ inches in depth of body cloth, slightly rounded  at front and fastened with one hook and eye, piped with facing cloth round the end and along the top, ½ inch black silk lace round the collar below the piping     Cuffs of body cloth 5½ inches deep in front piped with facing cloth and rounded off at hind arm seam, with piping carried down each side of seam finishing off ¾ inch from the bottom     Shoulder straps of body cloth, piped all round, except at base, with facing cloth     Eight large horn buttons, Rifle pattern, down front, two at skirt behind and two small horn buttons, Rifle pattern on shoulder straps     Sleeves and fronts lined with white cotton, waist hook in seam on both sides     A pocket up and down in side left breast

### 42nd DEOLI REGIMENT

182  As above, with following exceptions :

**Boots** —Ankle
**Leggings** —White ; khaki putties in marching order
**Great coat and Cape** —Regimental pattern

**H W Uniform**—Khaki with scarlet knickerbockers
**Knickerbockers**—As in para 178, but of serge, scarlet ordinary (optional, serge of Indian officers' quality)
**Sash**—Crimson silk
**Sword Belt**—Brown leather

### 43rd ERINPURA REGIMENT

**183.** As above, with the following exceptions :—
**Sash**—Not worn.
**Sword**—Light Cavalry pattern—Brown leather scabbard if provided regimentally

### REGIMENTS DRESSED IN DRAB

## British Officers

### Full Dress

**184 Helmet.**—As in para 29    The 28th Infy and 27th Punjabis, 33rd Punjabis 40th Pathans, 46th Punjabis wear silver plated ornaments
**Lace.**—Drab mohair
**Pouch**—Brown leather, regimental pattern    Badges as in Appendix I
**Pouch Belt**—Brown leather, 3 inches wide, with silver regimental plate, whistle and chain
**Scabbard**—Steel (20th Infy—Wooden scabbard covered with ass's skin, with steel mountings)
**Sword**—As in Appendix VIII
**Sword Belt**—Web as in Appendix 11(b)
**Sword Knot.**—Brown leather
**Trousers and Pantaloons**—Drab, with a single stripe of drab mohair lace 2 inches wide down the side seams
**Tunic.**—Drab, as for Regiments dressed in Green, with regimental facings Shoulder straps on tunic and mess jacket, Hussar pattern in drab, with badges of rank in silver

### Undress

**185 Forage Cap**—As in para 19
**Frock**—Drab as in para. 25
Other articles as in Full Dress    Pouch belt not worn

### Mess Dress

**186 Mess Jacket**—Drab, as for Regiments dressed in Green, with regimental facings, lined with drab silk.
**Mess Waistcoat.**—Drab, as for Regiments dressed in Green
*21st, 26th, and 27th Punjabis*—Scarlet cloth
*72nd and 92nd Punjabis.*—White washing
**Trousers**—As in Full Dress

### 124th AND 126th BALUCHISTAN INFANTRY

**187** As above, with the following exceptions :—

### Full Dress

**Buttons**—Gilt
**Horse Furniture**—Brown leather brow band and rosettes
**Lace**—Gold, ½ inch vellum
**Pouch Belt.**—Gilt regimental plate, whistle and chain
**Sword Belt, Sword Scabbard, and Sword Knot**—As for Regiments dressed in Scarlet.
**Trousers and Pantaloons.**—Red cloth, plain
**Tunic**—Drab cloth, pattern as for Regiments dressed in Scarlet, but with 2 pleats on skirts which are closed behind, with 2 buttons at waist ; scarlet edging on collar, down the front and on the pleats behind ; skirts and shoulder straps lined drab    Shoulder straps twisted round gold cord

*Mess Dress*

**188  Mess Jacket** —Drab cloth, or kerseymere, with collar and cuffs of regimental facings, gilt studs down the front, loop of gold braid to fasten across the throat, edged with gold braid, sleeve braided according to regimental pattern ; shoulder straps and badges of rank as for tunic

**Mess Waistcoat.**—Drab cloth, open, without collar ; gold braid edging round the top, down the front and along the bottom to the side seams ; pockets edged with gold braid forming crow's feet and eyes   A row of gilt studs and hooks and eyes down the front

**Trousers** —As in Full Dress

51st, 52nd, 53rd, AND 54th SIKHS ; 56th, 57th, 58th, AND 59th RIFLES

As above with the following exceptions :—

*Full Dress*

**189   Lace.**—Drab

**Pouch.**—Black leather, regimental pattern, with regimental number in silver on flap

**Pouch Belt.**—Brown leather (*56th and 59th Rifles*—Black patent leather) 3 inches wide, with silver plate, whistle and chain

**Scabbard** —Wooden, covered with ass's skin, coloured black, steel mountings, (*54th Sikhs and 57th Rifles*—Steel )

**Sword Belt** —Web, as in Appendix 11 (*b*)

**Sword Knot.**—Brown leather (*56th and 59th Rifles*—Black leather)

**Trousers and Pantaloons** —Drab cloth, with two stripes of drab mohair braid 1 inch wide, with a piping of the colour of the facings ½ inch wide between down the side seams   (*57th Wilde's Rifles*—Stripes of Lancer pattern )

**Tunic** —Drab cloth, edged all round, except the collar, with drab square cord, collar and cuffs the colour of the facings   The collar rounded in front and laced round the top with drab lace and plain edging of braid ; cuffs pointed ; a knot of square braid on the sleeve extending to 7 inches from the bottom of the cuff   The skirt rounded off in front   On each side of the breast 5 loops of drab square cord, with netted caps and drops, fastening with drab olivets, top loop 8 inches long, bottom one 4 inches   On each back seam a line of single cord forming a crow's foot at the top, passing under a netted cap at the waist, below which it is doubled, and ending in a knot at the bottom of the skirt   Shoulder straps of Hussar pattern in drab   Badges of rank in silver embroidery

*Mess Dress*

**190   Mess Jacket** —Drab cloth, edged all round with drab square cord ; collar and cuffs the colour of the facings   Plated studs, hooks and eyes down the front   Half inch mohair braid all round the collar trimmed through the centre with plumes and a row of small eyes along top edge ; on the sleeves a plain Austrian knot   Lining, drab silk   Shoulder straps and badges of rank as on tunic

*57th Wilde s Rifles* —Jacket cut and embroidered as for rifle regiments, but without silver studs ; no braid or hooks down the front

**Mess Waistcoat** - Open, without collar, of the colour of the facings (*51st Sikhs*—Drab cloth) edged all round with silver braid ; pockets edged with silver braid forming crow s feet and eyes at the corners ; plated studs and hooks and eyes down the front

*57th Rifles* —Closed and hooked up to the neck, with collar 1 inch high, of the colour of the facings, edged all round with gold braid ; pockets edged with gold braid

**Trousers** —As in Full Dress

*Horse Furniture*

**191   Universal Pattern** —Brow band and rosettes of the colour of the facings

## Indian Officers

**192   Boots** —Regimental pattern

**Great coat and Cape.**—Regimental pattern

**H W. Uniform and Service Dress** —Khaki, regimental pattern

**Knickerbockers.**—Serge, drab, ordinary (optional serge of Indian Officers' quality), cut loose with the looseness fitted into a waistband 2¼ inches wide to give plenty of room over the hips    The waist band is lined with cotton, grey, and fastened with a drawstring running through the centre    Fly fronted with three button holes and buttons    Bottoms loose and provided with a drawstring for fastening below the knee, string being covered as the knickerbockers are cut long enough to fall over about 4 inches

**Pagri.**—Regimental pattern

**Sword and Scabbard** —As in Appendix VIII

**Sword Belt, Knot, Pouch, and Pouch Belt.**—As for British officers

**Tunic** (*except 23rd Pioneers and Guides Infantry*) —Cloth, drab, super fine, with a piping of facing cloth ¼ inch wide down the left front, and from the bottom button to the bottom of tunic on the right front, also down centre of back skirt    Collar 1½ inches deep of facing cloth, slightly rounded at front and fastened with one hook and eye, with ¼ inch khaki silk lace round the ends and along the top    Shoulder straps of facing cloth with ¼ inch khaki silk lace all round except at base    Cuffs of facing cloth pointed 6½ inches deep in front and 2¼ inches at side and back ; ½ inch khaki silk lace all round showing ⅛ inch of facing cloth    Eight large buttons down front, two at skirt behind and two small buttons on shoulder straps    The sleeves and front are lined with white cotton    Waist hooks in seam on both sides    A pocket up and down inside left breast

### 9th BHOPAL INFANTRY

193   As above, with the following exceptions :—

*Full Dress*

**Sash.**—Crimson silk

*Undress*

194   The same as Full Dress but without gold lace and braid, and shoulder straps of chocolate instead of gold cord

### 23rd PIONEERS

195   As above with the following exception :—

**Blouse** —Serge, drab ordinary, length 40 inches to fit a man 5′ 9″ to 5′ 10″ varying 1½ inches for every 2 inches in height    Collar 1½ inches in depth of facing cloth, slightly rounded at front and fastened with one hook and eye, with ¼ inch khaki silk lace round the ends and along the top ; lined with drab Italian cloth    Shoulder straps of facing cloth with ¼ inch khaki silk lace all round except at base, fastened at neck with two small buttons    Cuffs of facing cloth 6½ inches deep in front and 2¼ inches at side and back, ½ inch khaki silk lace all round showing ⅛ inch of facing cloth    Opening in front 16½ inches in length made up 2½ inches wide, edged on both sides with ¼ inch of facing cloth, fastened in centre with three large buttons with a small hook and eye at top to fix to collar seam    Opening at side seam at bottom 6 inches in length    Kamarbands for wear with the blouse are of the colour of the regimental facings or khaki

### 51st SIKHS

196   As above with the following exception :—

**Pouch and Pouch Belt** —Regimental pattern

### 52nd, 53rd, AND 54th SIKHS ; 56th, 57th, 58th AND 59th RIFLES

197   As above, with the following exceptions :—

**Pouch and Pouch Belt.**—Regimental pattern

**Knickerbockers** —Khaki drill

### 106th HAZARA PIONEERS.

198   As above, with the following exception :—

**Knickerbockers** —Serge, drab ordinary ; regimental pattern (peg tops)

### 124th AND 126th BALUCHISTAN INFANTRY

199.  As above  with the following exceptions :—

**Knickerbockers.**—Serge red, ordinary ; regimental pattern (peg-tops)

**Leggings** —White canvas with cord loops

## PART X

SUPPLY AND TRANSPORT CORPS
### Officers permanently appointed to the Corps
### Officers above the Rank of Colonel
*Full Dress*

200   **Badges** —Gilt or gilding metal, corps pattern

**Buttons** —Gilt, corps pattern

**Helmet.**—Universal pattern with badge on pagri as for forage cap

**Lace** —Gold, staff pattern

**Plume** —White swan feathers drooping outwards, 8 inches long, with blue feathers under them long enough to reach to the ends of the white ones ; feathered stem 3 inches long

**Sash** —Gold and crimson silk net $2\frac{1}{4}$ inches wide ; two crimson stripes, $\frac{1}{4}$ inch wide the rest gold round tassels of gold fringe, 9 inches long

**Sword** —As for General Officer according to rank

**Sword Belt** —Web As in Appendix 11($b$)

**Sword Knot** —Gold and crimson cord and acorn

**Sword Slings** —Russia leather one inch wide, gold oak leaf lace $\frac{7}{8}$ inch wide.

**Trousers and Pantaloons** —Blue cloth with two white cloth stripes $\frac{3}{4}$ inch wide and $\frac{1}{2}$ inch apart down the side seams

**Tunic** —Blue cloth with white collar and cuffs    The collar laced all round the top and bottom with $\frac{3}{4}$ inch gold lace, a figured braiding of small eyes between the rows ; the cuffs pointed with two bars of $\frac{3}{4}$ inch gold lace round the top, showing $\frac{1}{4}$ inch of white cloth between the bars, a figured braiding of alter . nate large and small eyes above and below the lace    The top of the braided figure is 10 inches from the bottom of the cuff in front and 4 inches behind Eight buttons down the front    The front edged with white cloth $\frac{1}{4}$ inch wide The skirt rounded off in front, open behind half way to the waist, edged with white cloth with a three pointed flap on the back of each shirt edged with round gold cord, 3 buttons in each flap and two at the waist behind, lined with black silk    Shoulder cords as for General Officer

*Undress*

201   **Badge on Forage Cap** —The Royal Crest with crossed sword and baton in gold embroidery on blue cloth within a laurel wreath ; the blade of the sword in silver

**Forage Cap** —As in para 77

**Frock Coat** —Universal pattern as for General Officer according to rank, with buttons as for tunic

**Frock Serge** —Universal pattern    Red gorget patches    Corps buttons Other articles as in Full Dress

*Service Dress*

202   Universal pattern with red gorget patches as in para 78

*Mess Dress*

203   Corps pattern, as in para 206

### Other Officers
*Full Dress*

204   **Boots and Spurs** —As in paras 16 and 40

**Great coat.** —As in para 28

**Helmet** —As in para 29    Spike of bright gilt metal on a dead gilt base, leaf pattern

**Lace** —Gold, staff pattern, for tunic and mess jacket, and corps pattern with $\frac{1}{8}$ inch dark blue stripe in the centre for belts : on the slings the centre stripe is $\frac{1}{16}$ inch wide

**Pouch** —Black patent leather, collapsible, solid leather flap, reaching to the lower edge of the case    Gilt leaves for loops    For device, see Appendix I

**Pouch Belt** —Gold lace, 2 inches wide $\frac{1}{4}$ inch dark blue centre stripe, chased buckle tip and slide

**Sword and Scabbard** —As in Appendix VIII

**Sword Belt** —Gold lace, 1½ inches wide, with removable slings 1 inch wide; a swivel hook on eye of front sling for hooking up sword, running carriage for back sling; flat billets for sword slings with square wire buckles   Dark blue morocco leather lining

**Sword Knot** —Gold and blue cord and acorn

**Trousers and Pantaloons** —Blue cloth with two white cloth stripes ¾ inch wide, and ⅛ inch apart down the side seams

**Tunic.**— Blue with collar and cuffs of white cloth   Collar laced round the top with ¾ inch lace, with gold cord (similar to that in the shoulder straps) round bottom; cuffs pointed and ornamented with an Austrian knot of round-back gold cord   Eight buttons in front and two at waist behind   Skirts rounded off in front, open behind half way to waist edged with white cloth with a 3-pointed flap on the back of each skirt edged with round gold cord, 3 buttons on each flap and lined with black silk; white cloth edging ⅛ inch wide all round, except the collar, twisted round gold shoulder cords, lined with blue, small button of corps at the top

**Waist Plate.**—Gilt or gilding metal rectangular plate with corps device   As in Appendix I

*Undress*

205   **Forage Cap** —As in para 19

**Frock** —As in para 25, shoulder straps, white cloth with ½ inch blue light down the centre, with corps buttons

**Sword Belt.**—Web, as in Appendix 11 (*b*)

Other articles as in Full Dress   Pouch belt not worn

*Mess Dress*

206.   **Mess Jacket** —Blue cloth edged all round with ¾ inch gold lace, form ing a ring at the bottom of each back seam; white stand up collar and cuffs; a line of ¼ inch gold braid along the collar seam; cuffs pointed and edged with ¾ inch lace  the point extending to 6 inches from the bottom of the cuff, 2 inches deep at the back; a loop of gold braid at the bottom of the collar to fasten across the neck; a row of studs down the front on the left side; fastened with hooks and eyes : white silk lining   White cloth shoulder straps edged with ¼ inch lace

**Mess Waistcoat** —White washing, without lapels, fastened by four gilt buttons of corps pattern

**Trousers**—As in Full Dress

*Horse Furniture*

207   **Universal pattern** —Brow band and rosettes white

*Hot Weather Uniform and Service Dress*

208   Universal pattern as in General Instructions

209   Probationers and officers on the cadres of regiments employed with the Supply and Transport Corps may wear their regimental or Unattached List uniform and horse furniture only in Full Dress No 1, Mess Dress No 4, and Undress No 5   Hot weather uniform and service as in para 208  with the S and T Corps Gorget Patch described in para 27

## Commissioned Officers with Honorary Rank.

210   Uniform, etc , as for officers of their respective ranks

The provision of all articles of Full Dress and Mess Dress is optional, but officers should when granted first class passages on transports, where they will be associated with other officers, provide themselves with mess dress or evening dress for wear on board   The serge frock may be worn in lieu of the tunic

## Indian Officers of Transport Units

211  Indian officers of transport units may wear a Full Dress uniform of the following description but it is optional :—

**Belt** —Brown leather, 2 inches wide, with plain silver plate $2\frac{1}{3}$ by $2\frac{7}{8}$ inches, number of corps in gilt $\frac{3}{4}$ inch numbers  Brown leather sword slings, 1 inch wide, with square buckles of white metal

**Kullah.**—Red with gold embroidery

**Kamar band** —Red saloo with red and gold palloo

**Kurta** —Cavalry  pattern ; blue serge without facings, $\frac{1}{2}$ inch gold lace round top of collar  Thin gold tracings round bottom of collar and carried down both sides of the front, opening with three buttons ; buttons $\frac{1}{2}$ inch  round gilt  Shoulder cords plain cloth  with brass badges of rank ; $\frac{1}{2}$ inch gold lace round cuffs coming to a point

**Pagri** —Indian officer s Full Dress  blue and gold

**Pyjamas** —White, regimental  pattern

**Scabbard.**—Brown  with steel bands and rings

**Sword** —Straight, officers' pattern, light cavalry hilt

**Sword Knot** —Flat brown leather, $\frac{1}{4}$ inch, with acorn

**Shoes.**—Gurgabis

INDIAN MEDICAL SERVICE

## Surgeon General

212  Uniform as laid down for the Army Medical Service —(Dress Regulations for the Army, paras 902, *et seq* ), with the following exceptions : —
**Buttons** — I M S pattern
**Mess Jacket** —Blue cloth, edged all round with 1 inch gold lace, forming
a ring at the bottom of each back seam ; cuffs pointed and edged with 1 inch lace,
6 inches high at the point and $2\frac{1}{4}$ inches behind ; a loop of gold braid at bottom of
collar to fasten across the neck ; gilt studs down the front on the left side, fastened
with hooks and eyes ; scarlet silk lining ; plaited round gold shoulder cords of
plaited gold wire basket cord $\frac{3}{16}$ inch in diameter, small gold gimp down
centre, and small button at the top ; strap of the shoulder cord $2\frac{1}{4}$ inches wide
terminating in a 4 inch wing   Badges of rank in silver embroidery
**Mess Waistcoat.**—As for the A M S, or an alternative plain open white
washing waistcoat without lapels and fastened by 4 small gilt departmental
buttons

## Colonel
### *Full Dress*

213  **Boots.**—Mounted—Butcher   Dismounted—Wellington
**Gloves.**—As in para  26
**Great coat.**—Universal pattern, as in para  28
**Helmet.**—As in para  29
**Lace, Gold** —Staff pattern
**Plume.**—Black swan feathers drooping outwards 7 inches long
**Pouch.**—Black morocco leather, the flap 6 inches long and $3\frac{1}{4}$ inches deep with
3 stripes of gold embroidery $\frac{3}{8}$ inch wide round the bottom and sides   Badge as in
Appendix 1
**Pouch Belt** —Black morocco leather, 2 inches wide, with 4 stripes of gold
embroidery, each $\frac{3}{8}$ inch wide ; gilt chased buckle, tip and slide
**Spurs.**—As in para 40
**Sword and Scabbard** —As described in Appendix VIII with device of the
Royal and Imperial Cypher and Crown on hilt
**Sword Belt.**—Black morocco leather, $1\frac{1}{2}$ inches wide with slings 1 inch wide,
3 stripes of gold embroidery $\frac{3}{8}$ inch wide on belt and $\frac{3}{16}$ inch wide on slings
A gilt hook to hook up sword.
**Sword Knot** —Gold and black lace strap and acorn
**Trousers and Pantaloons.**—Blue cloth with scarlet stripe $1\frac{3}{4}$ inches wide
and welted at the edges down the side seams
**Tunic.**—Blue cloth, the skirt rounded off in front and closed behind   Black
velvet collar and cuffs, the collar ornamented with $\frac{3}{4}$ inch lace round the top,
gold Russia braid along the bottom and a figured braiding of alternate large and
small eyes below the lace the cuffs pointed with 2 bars of $\frac{3}{4}$ inch lace showing $\frac{1}{4}$
inch of black velvet between the bars, a figured braiding of alternate large and
small eyes above and of small eyes only below the lace, according to special
pattern, the top of the braided figure is 10 inches from the bottom of the cuff,
8 buttons down the front and 2 at the waist behind.  Scarlet cloth edging all
round (except the collar) and up the skirt pleats ; the skirts lined with black
silk, shoulder straps of twisted round gold cord universal pattern lined with blue,
small button at the top   Badges of rank in silver embroidery

### *Undress*

214  **Forage Cap** —As in para  19
**Frock** —As in para 25.
**Frock Coat, Universal** —As in para 24
Other articles as in Full Dress   Pouch belt not worn

### *Mess Dress*

215  **Mess Jacket.**—As for Surgeon General, but the lace is $\frac{3}{4}$ inch wide ;
a line of gold Russia braid along the bottom of the collar and shoulder straps
as for tunic

Queen Alexandra's Military Nursing Service

**Mess Waistcoat.**—Scarlet cloth closed to the throat; edged with $\frac{3}{16}$ inch gold Russia braid all round and on the collar seam. Pockets edged with similar braid forming a crow s foot at each end Gilt studs and hooks and eyes down the front; or an alternative plain open white washing waistcoat as laid down for Surgeon General

**Trousers**—As in Full Dress

### All other Officers

216 As for Colonel, with the following exceptions :—

**Plume**—Not worn

**Pouch**—Black morocco leather, collapsible, of special pattern to contain the regulation instrument case; the flap $6\frac{1}{2}$ inches long and 4 inches deep, with 2 stripes of gold embroidery $\frac{3}{8}$ inch wide round the bottom and sides Badge as in Appendix I

**Pouch Belt**—Three stripes of embroidery

**Swoid Belt and Slings**—Two stripes of embroidery

**Tunic**—The braided eyes on the collar and cuffs are omitted One bar of lace only on the cuffs

### Hot Weather Uniform and Service Dress

217 As in General Instructions

**Service Dress Jacket**—The open fronted pattern

**H W Mess Jacket**—The stand up collar

### Horse Furniture

218 **Universal pattern**—As in Appendix VI

## Queen Alexandra's Military Nursing Service for India

219 Winter—Grey Facings—Scarlet cashmere
Summer—White Facings—Scarlet twill cotton

**Apron**—White cambric (or linen), gored buttoning at back, length to bottom of skirt, square bib to cover third button from top of bodice, no straps, shaped pocket from waist band (for duty only).

**Belt**—Scarlet cashmere or twill 2 inches wide fastened with hooks and eyes, not studs.

**Bodice**—Grey beige, on lining, tight plain back with shaped seam in centre, drawing strings from sides, loose fronts with gathers, fulness coming from the neck band only; 8 scarlet bone buttons in front starting 1 inch from neck and $1\frac{3}{4}$ or 2 inches apart according to length, 1 inch plain piece for buttonholes; plain coat sleeve lined, opening at bottom 3 inches deep with 2 buttons $\frac{1}{2}$ inch and $2\frac{1}{2}$ inches from bottom and a scarlet cashmere band 2 inches wide sewn on 3 inches from bottom

White cambric (or drill) as above, but without tight back and shaped seam in centie and with the drawing strings from centre of back and facings of scarlet twill

Scarlet waistcoat and cuffs for Lady Superintendent

**Bonnet**—Grey straw, lined black silk, trimmed grey corded silk ribbon bow on top, edged grey velvet and white muslin frilling in front with white lawn tucked strings to tie in bow under chin

**Cap**—Dora, white Lace edging for Lady Superintendent

**Cape**—Grey beige, to elbow, piped grey, without collar and lined scarlet cashmere (for indoor wear only)

**Coat.**—Grey tweed, unlined, three quarter sacque, $3\frac{1}{2}$ inches below knee Side pockets and vents Grey fur, flannel or Italian cloth lining can be added to suit the climate

**Collars.**—Scarlet, cashmere or twill shaped $1\frac{1}{4}$ and $1\frac{3}{4}$ inches high sewn on to neck band No studs showing on scarlet collars

White linen guards' collars 2 inches high, worn inside the scarlet collar fastened on studs showing $\frac{1}{2}$ inch of the white

**Cuffs**—White $3\frac{1}{2}$ inches wide to be worn under the sleeves

**Hats** (*Optional*)—Sailor, white straw with white ribbon Sailor, grey beige covered frame

**Jewellery** —No jewellery to be worn with uniform

**Skirt**—Grey beige, lined, cut circular shape, plain on hips and inverted pleat at back, brush braid at foot.

White cambric (or drill) cut circular shape, plain on hips, gathered at back 3 inches, 6 inch hem with 1 inch tuck under same for shrinkage

Lady Nurses are required to wear uniform when on duty and when attending any official function  At military parades and reviews, a simple white pith hat may be worn with plain white scarf folded round  Mufti may be worn at all other times  When attending any evening function they may wear a dress of soft white silk with scarlet silk facings and covered buttons, made uniform pattern, except that skirts will have a train of 7 inches  White gloves will be worn. Caps will be worn of ordinary uniform pattern and made of fine lawn or muslin

Lady Nurses on appointment and returning from leave in England are required to wear uniform on reporting themselves at the staff office, Bombay or Karachi, and thereafter according to the regulations in force in India for the time being ; but during the voyage to India ordinary dress may be worn

## Indian Subordinate Medical Department
### Senior Sub Assistant Surgeons

220 **Boots** —Ankle

**Cap** —(*Eurasian Sub Assistant Surgeons*)— Dark blue  cloth without peak with mohair band 1¾ inches deep, mohair button on top, and metal crown in front  The crown to be moveable, and when a quilted cap cover of khaki with a flap to protect the back of the neck is used as a protection against the sun, the  crown  to be  attached  to the  cover  in front   Japanned leather chin strap ½ inch wide

**Great coat, Sword and Scabbard** —As  for  British  warrant  officers, I S. M D

**Pagri**—(For Sikhs) :—Yellow  pag, under a dark blue safa with gold ends Khaki safa with Service Dress ; badge the Royal Crest in silver.

**Kullah** —(Except for Sikhs)   Scarlet cloth with gold embroidery

**Lungi** —Dark blue cotton with gold work and gold fringe at both ends

**Pouch and Pouch Belt** —Black morocco leather without lace or stripe   The belt to be 2 inches wide with gilt chased buckle, tip and slide   The pouch (to hold a case of pocket instruments the same size as for Senior Assistant Surgeons) attached to the pouch by gilt swivels   The Royal and Imperial Cypher and Crown in gilt metal on the centre of the pouch

**Service Dress** —Universal pattern, but with stand-up collar fastened with two hooks and eyes   Sam Browne belts and scabbard  The letters "I S M D " are worn on  the shoulder straps of great coat and khaki uniform

**Shoes.**—Ordinary English pattern

**Sword Belt** —Black  morocco leather 1½ inches wide with  flap and gilt hook to hook up sword

**Trousers** —Dark blue cloth with scarlet stripe 1¼ inches wide  down  the side seams

**Tunic** —Dark blue cloth, scarlet edging all round, and up the skirt pleats ; collar of black velvet edged with ¼ inch gold lace round top and bottom Eight gilt buttons down the front, one on each shoulder, and two at the waist behind  Shoulder straps of black velvet rounded at top and edged with ½ inch gold lace, except at the base ; pointed cuffs of black velvet, 5 inches high at the point and 2½ inches behind, trimmed with ½ inch gold lace  Waist hooks to support the sword belt  Badges of rank in silvered metal on shoulder straps.

## Departmental Commissioned Officers with Honorary Rank

*(Except Supply and Transport Corps)*

*Full Dress*

221 **Boots.**—Wellington

**Gloves** —White leather

**Great coat** —As in para 28

**Helmet and Fittings.**—*Ordnance Department in India* —As for Royal Field Artillery — *I S M D* as for I M S   *All other Departments* as for officers of Infantry

**Lace** —Staff pattern.

**Pouch Belt and Pouch** —*Ordnance Department in India* —As for officers of the Army Ordnance Department

*Indian Subordinate Medical Department* —Black morocco leather, with stripe of gold embroidery $\frac{3}{8}$ inch wide, on each outer edge   The belt 2 inches wide with gilt chased buckle tip and slide   Pouch (to hold a case of pocket instruments) with flap $6\frac{1}{4}$ inches long and 4 inches deep attached to the pouch belt by gilt swivels

*Military Works Services, Barrack, Public Works, Telegraphs, and Sappers and Miners* —As for officers, R E

*All other departments.*—Belt, gold lace 2 inches wide, and pouch of black morocco with Royal and Imperial Cypher

**Sword and Scabbard.**—*Ordnance Department in India* —As for officers, R A

*All other Departments* —As for British Officers of Indian Infantry dressed in Scarlet

**Sword Belt and Knot** —*Ordnance Department in India* —As for officers of the Army Ordnance Department

*Indian Subordinate Medical Department* —As for officers I M S

*Military Works Services, Barrack, Public Works, Telegraphs and Sappers and Miners* —As for officers, R E

*All other departments.*—Belt, gold lace $1\frac{3}{4}$ inches wide with $\frac{1}{8}$ inch crimson silk stripe in centre   Knot—As for British Infantry

**Trousers** —*Ordnance Department in India* —Blue cloth, 2 scarlet stripes, $\frac{3}{4}$ inch wide and $\frac{1}{8}$ inch apart down the side seams.

*Army Clothing Department* —As above, but with light blue cloth stripes

*Army Remount Department* —As above, but with yellow stripes

*Military Farms Department.*—As above, but with 1 stripe of grass green cloth, $1\frac{3}{4}$ inches wide with $\frac{1}{8}$ inch scarlet light down the centre.

*Indian Subordinate Medical Department, Military Works, including Barrack, Public Works, Telegraph and Sappers and Miners, Garrison and Depôt Staff, Miscellaneous List, and Military Accounts* —As above, but with 1 stripe of scarlet cloth, $1\frac{3}{4}$ inches wide

*Superintendents, Detention Barracks* —As above, but with 1 stripe of black mohair lace $1\frac{3}{4}$ inches wide

**Tunic.**—*Ordnance Department in India* —Blue cloth   Collar of scarlet cloth $2\frac{1}{4}$ inches deep cut square in front, fastened with 2 black hooks and eyes, $\frac{5}{8}$ inch lace round the ends and along the top, and braid, gold No 1 along the bottom   The collar is lined with black silk; tab of buckram covered with black silk   Sleeves with pointed cuffs of scarlet cloth, 5 inches deep at the front and 2 inches at the sides   Above the cuff there is a row of lace $\frac{5}{8}$ inch extending to $7\frac{1}{2}$ inches from the bottom of the sleeve ; $\frac{3}{16}$ inch above the lace there is a row of braid, gold, No 1, which is formed into an Austrian knot on the top, extending to $9\frac{1}{4}$ inches from the bottom of the sleeves; $\frac{1}{16}$ inch below the lace there is a row of the same braid formed into a knot   Twisted gold shoulder knots, lined with blue cloth fastened to a small button at the top and at the bottom by a small hook, black spring, to a loop of black silk worked on the shoulder of the tunic   A piping of scarlet cloth, $\frac{3}{16}$ inch wide all round, similar piping at the centre of the skirt which is rounded at the bottom in front ; on either side of the centre of the skirt at the back there is a slash of blue cloth piped with $\frac{3}{16}$ inch scarlet   On this slash there are 3 large buttons   Body and sleeves lined with drab silk, skirt with black silk   Eight buttons down the front   In the waist seam on the left side there is a brass waist hook, a pocket—up and down—inside the left breast, top 3 inches from top of forepart, opening $6\frac{1}{4}$ inches long

*Army Clothing Department* —As for the Ordnance, but with light blue cloth collar, cuffs, and piping

*Army Remount Department* —As above, but with yellow cloth collar, cuffs and piping

*Military Farms Department* —As for the Miscellaneous List, but with grass-green cloth collar and cuffs.

*Indian Subordinate Medical Department.*—As for the Ordnance, but with black silk velvet collar and cuffs   Scarlet piping ⅛ inch wide round the edges, up the centre of the skirt at the back, and round the slashes.

*Military Works Departments including Barrack, Public Works, Telegraph, and Sappers and Miners* —As for the Miscellaneous List but with piping of blue cloth

*Miscellaneous List, and Military Accounts* —Scarlet cloth, cut similar to the Ordnance Department except that the front of the skirt is square Collar and cuffs of blue cloth.  The collar is lined with white cloth, the shoulder straps with scarlet cloth and fastened at the bottom to a loop of scarlet silk on the shoulder of the tunic   The slashes are of scarlet cloth and the piping is white   Body and sleeves lined with drab silk, skirt with white cloth which is left open along the bottom   The braid below the lace on the sleeves is formed into a small eye in the centre instead of into a knot as for the Ordnance Department

*Superintendents, Detention Barracks* —As for the Miscellaneous List, but with black cloth collar and cuffs

*Undress (all Departments)*

**222   Forage Cap** —As in para  19.

**Frock** —As in para 25, with shoulder straps of the colour of the facings

**Gloves** —Brown leather.

Other articles as in Full Dress

*Service Dress*

**223   Boots** —Ankle —As in para  16

**Breeches** —As in para  17

**Helmet** —As in para  29

**Jacket** —As in para  31   The I S M D. wear the open fronted pattern

**Leggings or Putties** —As in paras 32 and 35

**Shoulder Strap Titles.**—The following distinctive letters are worn on the shoulder straps of khaki jackets and great coats by departmental officers with honorary rank :—

| | |
|---|---|
| Army Remount Department | A R |
| Garrison Depôt and Musketry Staff, Chief Instructors of Central Gymnasia | G R. I |
| Indian Subordinate Medical Department | I S M D |
| Military Farms Department | Farms |
| Military Prisons and Detention Barracks | M P. |
| Military Works Services (including Barrack) | M W |
| Miscellaneous Departments, except as provided elsewhere | Staff |
| Ordnance Department in India | O |
| Public Works Department, Conductors of Sappers and Miners | R E |
| Supply and Transport Corps (except Officer Commanding Transport units who wear the number of their unit with the letters " T C ", e g , 28 T C) | S T C |

*Mess Dress*

**224   Boots** —Wellington

**Mess Jacket** —*Ordnance Department in India.*—Blue serge, No I, lined throughout with drab or scarlet mercerised cotton ; roll collar of scarlet cloth  No I, shoulder straps of the same material as the garment   Sleeves with pointed cuffs of scarlet cloth 6 inches deep at the front and 2½ inches at the sides

*Army Clothing Department.*—As above, but with light blue cloth facings

*Army Remount Department* —As above, but with yellow cloth collar and cuffs

*Military Farms Department* —As for the Miscellaneous List, but with grass green collar and cuffs

*Indian Subordinate Medical Department* —As above, but with black silk velvet collar and cuffs

*Miscellaneous List and Military Accounts, Military Works Services (including Barrack, Public Works, Telegraph, and Sappers and Miners) and Garrison and Depôt Staff* —As above, except that the garment is made of scarlet serge No I and the collar and cuffs are of blue cloth

*Superintendents, Detention Barracks* —As for the Miscellaneous List, but with black cloth collar and cuffs

**Mess Waistcoat** —White pique fastened with 4 small buttons, 2 pockets

225 The provision of all articles of Full and Mess Dress is optional, but officers should, when granted first class passages on transports, where they will be associated with other officers, provide themselves with Mess Dress or evening dress for wear on board    The serge frock may be worn in lieu of the tunic

## Appointments for which no special uniform is prescribed

*Army Clothing, Cantonment Magistrates, Judge Advocate General's, Military Accounts, Military Farms Departments etc*

226 Officers holding such appointments will wear the uniform of their regiment or corps without addition or alteration.   When struck off the cadres of their units, they will wear the uniform of the Indian Army prescribed in para 231

### Army Remount Department

227 Officers on the cadres of units—Regimental uniform    Officers not on the cadres of units wear the uniform of the unit in which they last served    This also applies to Indian officers

### Chaplains of the Churches of England and Scotland

228 **Service Dress, Khaki,** as prescribed in these regulations will be worn on active service with a badge in black metal a cross patée on a plain metal tablet surmounted by a crown on the shoulder strap, and gorget patch of green cloth with loop of black Russia braid tracing down the centre of the patch, with a gilt stud near the point  No sword or belt

**Field Cap** —Khaki, Austrian pattern

### Inspectors of Army Schools

229  As prescribed in Dress Regulations for the Army, paras  1312 to 1335 *et seq*

### Officers in Civil Employ.

230  A military officer who is appointed substantively to any civil office for which uniform is prescribed shall wear the uniform of that office

On all State and other occasions when military officers wear uniform, military officers who are in permanent civil employ but who do not hold an appointment which carries the right to wear civil uniform may, at their option, wear the uniform of the corps or department to which they belonged or plain clothes, but officers appointed temporarily or permanently to the Survey of India or Cantonment Magistrates Department will wear military uniform in all orders of dress

Military officers who are temporarily in civil employ shall wear their military uniform, but may, if they desire, wear plain clothes instead of mess uniform, on occasions when the latter is worn by officers in military employ    An officer employed as private secretary to the Viceroy, a Governor or a Lieutenant Governor, will wear military uniform

### Officers of the Indian Army not on the Cadre of a Unit

231  Uniform and horse furniture as for Infantry Regiments  Dressed in Scarlet with following exceptions :—

**Facings.**—Blue

**Lace** —Gold staff pattern

Tunic —Cuffs pointed, with ½ inch lace round the top extending to 9½ inches from the bottom of the cuff, and a tracing of gold Russia braid ¼ inch below the lace

## Native Indian Land Forces and Indian Officers with Honorary Rank in the Army

232 Uniform and horse furniture as prescribed in para 231 with the following modification : —

A white lungi may be worn instead of a white helmet and a khaki safa in place of a khaki helmet  A white lungi, without aigrette may be worn at the option of the officer in mess dress  The staff aiguillette frock coat and gorget patches and a red and white aigrette will be worn by officers serving on the staff  The aigrette is worn with the lungi, when British staff officers wear the plume with the helmet, and is fastened to the lungi by means of a brooch badge bearing the Royal and Imperial Cypher  The following is the description of the aigrette—Red and white egret's feathers, the red outside the white  The length of the red feathers 6 inches, and of the white 12 inches  The base where the feathers are bound together to be not more than 1½ inches round

### Civilians of Departments on Field Service

(a) *Civilians ranking with commissioned officers in the army*

233 Service Dress —As prescribed in these regulations with the following exceptions :—

Field Cap —Khaki, Austrian pattern

Gorget Patch —2¼ inches long and 1¼ inches wide, pointed at the outer end, sewn on to each side of the collar, of green cloth with a loop of black Russia tracing down the centre and a gilt stud at the point  Civilians employed with departments which have a departmental gorget patch will wear it instead of the green one

Badges of rank as for officers of corresponding army rank with brass distinctive letters below as follows :—

Acc —for Mily Accts Dept ;  Post —for Postal ;  Ry —for Railway;  Sur —for Survey ;  Tel —for Telegraph

Sword and Scabbard —Any pattern

(b) *Indian subordinates ranking with Indian officers*

Aims and Equipment —As for European subordinates

Uniform.—Service Dress blouse, knickerbockers or pyjamas, with khaki putties and ankle boots or native shoes; khaki pagri, or khaki cover to ordinary head dress

### Officers of the Unattached List awaiting admission to the Indian Army

234 As prescribed in Dress Regulations for the Army, paras 1419 to 1430

### Unemployed Officers

235 An unemployed general officer on the active list will wear the uniform of his rank

Unemployed officers of the late Indian Artillery or Engineers may, while in receipt of full pay, wear the uniform of their former regiment or corps

Unemployed officers (other than general officers) of the Indian Army, the local services and general lists, on vacating a staff, departmental or regimental appointment, may, until restored or re employed, wear the uniform of the unit or department in which they last served, or the uniform prescribed for the Indian Army

### Reserve of Officers, Indian Army

236 Officers of the Indian Army Reserve when employed on aimy duty will provide themselves with service dress and undress and mess dress of the

pattern worn in the unit or department to which they are attached    The letters "I A. R " will be worn below the badges of rank, in similar material to those badges

Officers are not required to provide themselves with uniform until their services are actually required, but they are authorised, when not in the perform ance of duty with the Volunteer Force or in a Government Department for which a special uniform is prescribed, to wear the uniform prescribed for infantry of the line with the letters "I A R " on the shoulder straps in similar material to the badges of rank, with the following exceptions :—

**Facings.**—Blue

**Lace** —Gold, two vellum

**Buttons.**—Gilt, burnished, with crown and scalloped edge

**Forage Cap** —Badge, Royal Cypher and Crown embroidered in gold

Officers who join the reserve of officers on resigning their active commissions are entitled to wear the uniform of the unit or department in which they last served, with the letters I A R on the shoulder straps as above, until removed from the reserve of officers on reaching the age limit

Officers of the Indian cavalry reserve called up for training will wear the uniform of the volunteer corps to which they belong

## Retired Officers *

237  All officers retired from the active list may wear the uniform of the unit or department in which they last served, but with the letter R on the shoulder cords or shoulder straps below the badges of rank

General officers will wear the uniform of their rank, with a plain gold sash $2\frac{1}{2}$ inches wide, without crimson stripes, round the waist

Retired Indian officers may wear the uniform of the unit or corps in which they last served    Those who continue to attend Durbars after retirement, in virtue of their military rank, should wear the uniform of that rank

Gold and silver laced trousers and overalls which were authorised prior to February 1902, are no longer to be worn by retired military officers of any branch of the service, who are privileged to wear uniform    Trousers and overalls of the description now laid down for the respective Services will be worn

---

* Unemployed or retired officers whose last appointment was one for which a special staff uniform is prescribed will wear either the uniform prescribed for their rank in the Indian Army or that of the regiment in which they last served

# APPENDIX I

## UNIFORM; FACINGS; BADGES AND DEVICES

Staff officers wearing regimental uniform —Regimental badges and devices except on forage cap on which the Royal Crest in gold embroidery is worn

**Personal Appointments to the Viceroy** —*Uniform* red ; *facings* blue. *Badges and Devices* —*On buttons* —The Garter surmounted by a Tudor crown ; within the Garter, the Royal Cypher    *On tunic.*—The lotus leaf *On waistplate.*—In silver the Royal Cypher and Tudor crown encircled with oak leaves ; on the bottom of the wreath a scroll inscribed *Dieu et mon droit*

**Indian Army** —*Uniform* red ; *facings* blue    *Badges and Devices* —*On buttons* —The Royal and Imperial Cypher within a circle inscribed   Indian Army " with the Tudor crown above.   *On field cap* —As on buttons the whole encircled by a laurel wreath

**Officers of the U. L awaiting admission to the I. A** —*Uniform* red ; *facings* blue   *Badges and Devices* —*On buttons* —Gilt, burnished, with Tudor crown and scalloped edge    *On forage cap* —Royal and Imperial Cypher and Tudor crown in gilt metal

**Indian Army Reserve of Officers** — *Uniform* red ; *facings* blue   *Badges and Devices* — *On buttons.*—Gilt burnished unmounted, with Tudor crown and scalloped edge   *On forage cap.*—Royal Cypher and Tudor crown .embroidered in gold

**Supply and Transport Corps** —*Uniform* blue ; *facings* white   *Badges and Devices* —*On buttons* —Within a circle inscribed   Supply and Transport Corps " the Royal and Imperial Cypher   Above the circle a Tudor crown   *On collar of tunic.*—In silver, an eight pointed star surmounted by a Tudor crown. On the star in gilt or gilding metal, a laurel wreath Within the wreath on a white enamelled ground, the Garter and motto ; within the Garter, the initials of the corps in monogram    *On waist plate.*—In silver on a gilt or gilding metal rectangular plate, the Royal and Imperial Cypher and Tudor crown within a laurel wreath Below the wreath a scroll inscribed *Dieu et mon droit*    *On forage and field cap* —In silver, as on collar of tunic, but with corps monogram on a black enamelled ground    *On pouch.*—The Royal and Imperial Cypher and Tudor crown in gilt metal

**Indian Medical Service.**—*Uniform* blue ; *facings* black velvet. *Badges and Devices.*—*On buttons* —On a star a circle surmounted by a Tudor crown. The circle inscribed " Indian Medical Service "   Within the circle the Royal and Imperial Cypher. *On waist plate* —The Royal Crest in silver. *On field cap and forage cap* —The Royal Crest (Surgeon General, in gold embroidery the Royal Crest with crossed sword and baton, the blade of the sword in silver within a laurel wreath)   *On pouch and pouch belt* —The Royal and Imperial Cypher and Tudor crown in gilt

**I S M D** —*Uniform* blue ; *facings* black velvet    *Badges and Devices* —*On buttons* —Tudor crown and laurel wreath with Royal and Imperial Cypher.   *On waist plate* —Royal Crest in silver on centre piece and on outer circle the words ' Sub Medical Department " in silver.   *On forage cap.*—The Royal and Imperial Cypher and laurel wreath, and Tudor crown embroidered in gold on a blue cloth ground   *On pouch* —The Royal and Imperial Cypher and Tudor crown in gilt metal.

**Departmental Commissioned and Warrant Officers** (*except those of the S and T Corps who wear the badges and devices authorised for the officers of that corps*)   Ordnance — *Uniform* blue ; *facings* scarlet   Army Remount.—*Uniform* blue ; *facings* yellow   Army Clothing —*Uniform* blue ; *facings* white    Miscellaneous List and Military Accounts, Military Works (including Barrack, Public Works, Telegraphs, and Sappers and Miners)— *Uniform* scarlet , *facings* blue.   Military Prisons and Detention Barracks—*Uniform* scarlet ; *facings* black   Military Farms Department —*Uniform* scarlet ; *facings* grass green

*Badges and Devices. On buttons.*—G R I with laurel wreath and Tudor crown.   Ordnance —Gilt metal    The Indian Ordnance Department arms ;—above the shield, the Royal and Imperial Crown    Below the shield, the words   Ordnance India   within a scroll *On forage cap* —The Royal and Imperial Cypher   Ordnance —Gilt metal with vertical shank ; the Indian Ordnance Department arms.   On waist plate —The Royal and Imperial Cypher and Crown on the centre piece, and the word ' Unattached " on the outer circle   Both in silver.   Ordnance.—The Indian Ordnance Department arms, the words " Ordnance India " on the outer circle   Military Works, Barracks, Public Works, Telegraph, Sappers and Miners —As for Officers R. E    *Pouch* —The Royal and Imperial Cypher. Ordnance —As for officers, Royal Artillery   Military Works, Barracks, Public Works Telegraph, and Sappers and Miners —As for Officers, R E   *On collar* —Ordnance —Badge as described above, but of gilt metal Device. —Same as for cap badge.

**Viceroy's Bodyguard** —*Uniform* red ; *facings* blue   *Badges and Devices.*— *On buttons.*—*British officers.*—Gilt burnished, with the Royal and Imperial Cypher in a Garter, bearing the motto of the Order of the Garter and a Tudor crown above *Indian officers* — Brass , with crossed lances ; Tudor crown in upper angle and   G G B G " across the lower angle   *On field cap* —A Tudor crown in gold embroidery   *On forage cap.*—Tudor crown surmounted by a lion, passant, regardant, in gold embroidery   *On pouch* —In gold embroidery the monogram ' G G B G " surmounted by a Tudor crown   *On pouch belt* —Gilt burnished, side prickers and chains

**Governor's Bodyguard, Madras** —*Uniform* scarlet ; *facings* blue  *Badges and Devices* — On field cap— G B G' in gold embroidery on a dark blue ground  On pouch and pouch belt —(British officers only)—Brass Royal and Imperial Cypher surmounted by a Tudor crown.

**Governor's Bodyguard, Bombay.**—*Uniform* scarlet ;*facings* blue —*Badges and Devices* — On buttons —In brass "B B. G" in monogram surmounted by a Tudor crown  On waist plate —A Tudor crown in white metal on a brass plate  On pouch and pouch belt —In gilt, the Royal and Imperial Cypher

**1st Duke of York's Own Lancers (Skinner's Horse).**- *Uniform* yellow ;*facings* black velvet *Badges and Devices.*—On buttons —In gilt crossed lances bearing pennons ; in upper angle " 1 "; in lower the York rose ; round the edge the words ' Duke of York's Own Lancers ". Without inscription for undress  On waist plate —A gilt frosted square plate with raised silver crossed lances bearing pennons  Monogram  D Y O. " in centre with ' 1 above and York rose below  On forage cap —In gilt crossed lances bearing pennons with 1 ' in upper angle and silver York rose in lower  On field cap —As on forage cap  On pouch — In gilt crossed lances bearing pennons. In centre monogram  D Y O " with 1' above, and silver York rose below  Below a gilt scroll inscribed " Skinner s Horse "  Pouch belt — On a silver star the monogram  D Y O " and a scroll inscribed  The help of God and bravery of man  Over the monogram a mounted lancer and a scroll bearing in Urdu characters the same motto  Above the star a Tudor crown.  Above the crown a scroll inscribed  Skinner s Horse  Below the star scrolls bearing the honorary distinctions of the regiment  All in silver

**2nd Lancers (Gardner's Horse)** —*Uniform*  blue ; *facings* light blue  *Badges and Devices* —On buttons —In brass, double crossed lances bearing pennons ; in upper angle ' 2 "; in lower angle  the letter ' L  On waist plate —In white metal  as on buttons  On field cap —In silver as on buttons  On pouch and pouch belt —In gilt as on buttons

**3rd Skinner s Horse** — *Uniform* blue ; *facings* yellow  No devices

**4th Cavalry** —*Uniform* scarlet ; *facings* blue  *Badges and Devices* —The universal " Bengal Lancer' button  On helmet, field cap and forage cap —Silver crossed lances bearing pennons, surmounted by a Tudor crown. Above the crown a lion *passant re gardant.*  The numeral  IV  in lower angle  Below a frosted scroll inscribed ' Scinde 1844 " On pouch and pouch belt.—As on forage cap on a silver background

**5th Cavalry** —*Uniform* scarlet ;*facings* blue  *Badges and Devices* — On waist plate — In silver the figure  5 ' intertwined with the letter " C," with scroll at sides and below inscribed  Punjab,  Mooltan,"  Afghanistan 1879 80  The whole surmounted by a Tudor crown  On forage cap — ' 5  surmounted by a Tudor crown.  Below a scroll inscribed  Cavalry "  On the pouch —In gold embroidery on blue cloth, the monogram ' 5 C " sur mounted by a Tudor crown  Scroll at sides and below inscribed  Punjab," Mooltan,' "Afghanistan 1879 80. ' A wreath of laurel leaves in gold embroidery round edge of pouch

**6th King Edward's Own Cavalry** —*Uniform* blue ; *facings* scarlet  *Badges and Devices* —On buttons.—Gilt metal charged with the plume of the Prince of Wales in silver, surmounted with the Imperial Crown ; the Roman numerals ' V ' and  I" on left and right of plume, the monogram  K. E O C  at base  On collar of tunic, and kurta.— The plume of the Prince of Wales'; plume silver, coronet gilt.  On waist plate ...Gilt surcharged with the Royal and Imperial Cypher of King Edward VII wreathed with oak leaves ; the badge silver  On forage and field caps —The Royal and Imperial Cypher of King Edward VII, the crown gilt the Cypher blue enamelled and a scroll below, red enamelled ' 6th K E 'O. Cavalry "  On pouch—Scarlet cloth charged with the Royal and Imperial Cypher of King Edward VII, the Crown gilt, the monogram silver with  VI Cavalry " at the base, the whole enwreathed with gold embroidery bearing silver embroidered scrolls containing the honorary distinctions of the regiment

**7th Hariana Lancers** —*Uniform* scarlet ;  *facings* blue.  *Badges and Devices* —On field and forage caps —In gilt,  VII " surmounted by a Tudor crown in the centre of crossed lances  Silver pouch "—In gilt as  on field cap, but below number, a scroll inscribed " Hariana Lancers "

**8th Cavalry** —*Uniform* blue ; *facings* scarlet  On forage and field caps —In gilt crossed lances and pennons with " 8 " over crossing  The whole surmounted by a Tudor crown.  On pouch and pouch belt —In silver the Royal and Imperial Cypher surmounted by a Tudor crown.

**9th Hodson's Horse** —*Uniform* blue ; facings white —*Badges and Devices* —On buttons —In brass, crossed lances with pennons ;  9 " in upper angle and the letters ' H. H " over crossing of lances  On helmet and field cap —In silver crossed lances and pennons ; ' 9 " over crossing and scroll below joining handles of lances inscribed ' Hodson's Horse ' On waist plate  In silver (brass for Indian officers) crossed lances with pennons  Between lance points a Tudor crown ; ' 9 ' over the crossing  A scroll below inscribed  Hodson Horse '  On forage cap.—As on waist plate  On the pouch —In gold as on waist plate  On pouch belt —Silver side prickers in sheath with chains.

**10th Duke of Cambridge's Own Lancers (Hodson's Horse)** —*Uniform* blue ; *facings* scarlet  *Badges and Devices* —On buttons —Crossed lances with  10 ' in relief surmounted by a Tudor crown  The whole in brass  On waist plate and pouch —Crossed lances

in brass with " 10 ' in white metal in relief   The whole surmounted by a Tudor crown
On field cap —' X   in silver
  **11th  King Edward's Own Lancers (Probyn's Horse)** —*Uniform* blue ; *facings* scarlet
*Badges  and  Devices — On  buttons* —In gilt crossed  lances  with   pennons.   The
Prince of Wales' plume and motto over crossing   XI " in lower angle   *On helmet* —
Crossed lances with ' XI " in lower angle (in brass)   Prince of Wales' plume covering
brass angles (in silver)   *On waistplate* —Monogram   K  E.  O " over crossed lances,
Prince of Wales plume in upper angle ;   XI ' in lower angle (in silver on brass plate)
*On  forage and field  caps* —As on helmet (all in silver)   *On pouch.*—As on waistplate in
silver on silver pouch   *On pouch belt* —In silver  the  Prince of Wales' plume and motto
between the silver plates for the prickers and chains   *On the shoulder straps* —The Prince
of Wales' Plume, instead of numerals.
  **12th Cavalry** —*Uniform* blue ;  *facings* blue   *Badges and Devices.—On waist plate* —
In gilt, the  Royal and Imperial Cypher and Tudor crown   Oak wreath on each side and
scroll below inscribed  *Dieu et mon droit*   *On field cap* —Tudor crown over two crossed
swords and   XII " beneath.   *On pouch and pouch belt.*—In gilt   Tudor crown over two
crossed swords and ' XII ' beneath   Side scrolls inscribed   Abyssinia   Charasia",
" Peiwar Kotal "   Kabul 1879 ; '  below the   XII " a scroll inscribed   Afghanistan
1878 80   The whole surrounded by a laurel wreath
  **13th Duke of Connaught's Lancers (Watson's Horse)** —*Uniform* blue ;  *facings* scarlet.
*Badges and Devices — On buttons* - In white metal crossed lances with pennons with ' 13 "
over the crossing.   *On waist plate.*—In silver on a brass plate a device as on the buttons
*On field cap* —In silver as on buttons   *On the pouch* —In gilt as on buttons
  **14th Murray's Jat Lancers** —*Uniform* blue ; *facings* scarlet   *Badges and Devices.—On*
*buttons* —*Full dress* —In brass  crossed  lances bearing pennons ; in upper angle a Tudor
crown ; in side angles the numerals   1 " and ' 4 " Below, a scroll inscribed  Murrays Jat
Lancers "   *Undress* —Crossed lances bearing pennons ; a Tudor crown in the upper angle and
' XIV   in the lower.   *On helmet forage cap and field cap* —In silver,   crossed lances
bearing pennons ; ' XIV ' across the crossing of the lances   *On waist plate.*—British officers
—As on helmet ; Indian officers —In brass  the letters   M J L " with   XIV ' above.
  **15th Lancers (Cureton's Multanis.)**—*Uniform* blue ;   *facings* scarlet   *Badges  and*
*Devices —On waist plate* —Full dress —In silver  crossed lances with pennons and   15 "
over the crossing   *On forage cap* —In gilt  crossed lances and pennons   Over crossing
a star   On the star   15 "   Below a crescent inscribed ' Cureton's Multanis   *On field*
*cap.*—In gilt, as on  waist plate   *On pouch and pouch belt* — In silver, as on forage cap.
  **16th Cavalry** —*Uniform* blue ;  *facings* blue   *Badges and Devices —On buttons.*—Two
crossed lances enclosing a Tudor crown between pennons and ' XVI ' between butts   At
crossing of lances the letter   C   *On waist plate field cap and pouch* —As on buttons
  **17th Cavalry** —*Uniform* blue ;  *facings* white   *Badges and Devices —On buttons* —
XVII ' over a star and crescent ; below ' Cavalry   *On waist plate* —Star and crescent
over   XVII "   Below a scroll inscribed  Cavalry   *On field cap* —A silver star and
crescent over ' XVII "   *On pouch* —Star and crescent over ' XVII "   *On pouch belt* —As
on pouch, silver plate side prickers and chains.
  **18th King  George's Own Lancers** —*Uniform* scarlet ;  *facings* white   *Badges and*
*Devices —On buttons* —In brass crossed lances with pennons  18 ' surmounted by crown
in upper angle,   G R I " in centre, ' King George's Own Lancers   on scroll below   *On*
*forage and field cap* —In silver gilt as on buttons   *On pouch and pouch belt* —In silver gilt,
as on buttons
  **19th Lancers (Fane's Horse)** —*Uniform* blue ;  *facings* French  grey   *Badges and*
*Devices — On buttons* —Tunic and mess jacket —German silver crossed lances  with pennons
Other garments —German silver crossed lances with pennons   19 " inside angles of crossing.
*On waist plate and pouch* —Silver monogram   F H ' surmounted by a Tudor crown   *On*
*field cap* —In silver as on buttons of  other garments "   *On pouch belt.*—In silver, in
centre on an ornamental eight pointed star fastened on which is a plain oval band, inscribed
' Lancers Fane's Horse " and ' XIX ' in centre   Above this a Tudor crown, and above the
crown a scroll inscribed ' Fanes Horse—1860 "   Above this scroll a silver ornament, from
which hang two chains   Below the centre ornament a scroll inscribed " Taku Forts " " Pekin "
Below this, silver side prickers
  **20th Deccan Horse** — *Uniform*  rifle green ;   *facings*   white   *On  buttons* —British
officers —Gilt metal with   D H. in monogram   (Plain round gilt buttons on full dress
Kurta and with khaki)  Indian officers   Plain brass   *On forage cap* —A silver horse rampant
with a scroll below inscribed   Deccan '   *On pouch and pouch belt* — 'D. H ' in gilt
monogram.
  **21st Prince Albert Victor's Own Cavalry (Frontier Force) (Daly's Horse)** —*Uniform*
blue ; *facings* scarlet.   *Badges and Devices — On waist plate* —In silver on a brass plate
21 '  with a scroll below inscribed   Daly's Horse ' and one above inscribed  P A. V O.
Cavalry  Frontier Force '  and surmounted by a Tudor crown   *On forage cap and field*
*cap* —In gilt  21 '  over crossed swords hilts downwards, surmounted by a Tudor crown
Below, a scroll inscribed   P A V O. Cavalry, F F " *On pouch.*—British officers —As on
waist plate   Indian officers —As on waist plate but surrounded by laurel leaves and scrolls
inscribed ' Delhi,"   Lucknow " ' Afghanistan 1878 80," Ahmed Khel '

22nd Sam Browne's Cavalry (Frontier Force) —*Uniform* scarlet ; *facings* blue     *Badges and Devices.*—*On field cap* —On a red ground in brass a Tudor crown over "22" encircled by a wreath ; below the number a scroll inscribed     Sam Browne's   Cavalry'     *On the pouch* —In gold,   S. B  C" surmounted by a Tudor crown below   XXII"   The whole surrounded by a gold laurel wreath having a scroll entwined with the words in gold letters 'Delhi"   Afghanistan 1878 80"   Frontier Force"   Ahmed Khel     Lucknow"

23rd Cavalry (Frontier Force) —*Uniform* blue ; *facings* scarlet     *Badges and Devices*— *On waist plate* (Indian officers only)  In silver the Royal and Imperial Cypher surmounted by a Tudor crown with an oak wreath on either side. *On field cap* —The Kandahar star in bronze ; in the centre   XXIII     *On the pouch* —In gold embroidery, the monogram  F. F" surmounted by a Tudor crown   Below, monogram ' 23" with scrolls 'Kandahar 1880, F F Cavalry,'   Afghanistan, 1879 80"

25th Cavalry (Frontier Force) — *Uniform* dark green ; *facings* scarlet   *Badges and Devices* —*On waist plate.* —British officers— ' 25' surmounted by a Tudor crown ; below a scroll in scribed   Cavalry Frontier Force   Indian officers —As above in white metal   *On field cap* —In brass   XXV ' below scroll inscribed   Cavalry Frontier Force'   *On pouch* —In gilt, as on waist plate but with the addition of a gold laurel wreath crossed by scrolls inscribed ' Delhi '   Lucknow,'   'Charasia'   Afghanistan, 1878 80"   Kabul, 1879"

26th King George's Own Light   Cavalry —*Uniform* French grey ;   *facings* buff *Badges and Devices* —*On buttons.*—Silver, crossed lances behind Prince of Wales' plume with   L" and  ' C  in side angles and ' 26" in lower angle   *On collar of tunic* — Crossed lances bearing pennons, in the upper angle the Prince of Wales' plume in the lower angle the Royal and Imperial Cypher surmounted by a Tudor crown ; at crossing a scroll inscribed   26 K G O Light Cavalry." The whole in silver   *On shoulder* —The figures and letters   26 L C.' with smaller letters   K. G. O. between them below the Prince of Wales plume   The Prince of Wales plume and the letters ' K G O " in silver and the rest in brass for British officers ; the whole in brass for other ranks   *On forage and field cap.*—As for collar badge,   *On pouch and pouch belt,*—Royal and Imperial Cypher,

27th Light Cavalry — *Uniform* French grey ;  *facings* buff   *Badges and Devices.*— *On buttons* — 27  on crossed lances, surmounted by a Tudor crown ; below the letters 'L C. *On field cap* —Monogram   L C ' with   27" across it   *On pouch* —Gilt raised double Royal and Imperial Cypher  surmounted by a Tudor crown.   *On pouch belt.*—Silver scrolls "Carnatic '  Sholinghur,"  'Mysore"  ' Seringapatam," "Burma, 1885—87 side prickers and chains

28th Light Cavalry —*Uniform* French grey ;  *facings* buff.   *Badges and Devices*—*On buttons forage cap, and field cap* —Crossed swords with ' 28" in lower angle in silver *On pouch* —Gilt raised double Royal and Imperial Cypher surmounted by a Tudor crown *On pouch belt* —Silver side prickers and chains and scrolls inscribed "Mysore,' " Seringa patam,'  ' Mahidpore"

29th Lancers (Deccan Horse) —*Uniform* rifle green ; *facings* white     *Badges and De vices* —*On field cap* —In brass, crossed lances with pennons; '29 ' in side angles ;   D H' in lower angle     *On pouch* — Gilt metal crossed lances with pennons     *On pouch belt* — Silver engraved buckle tip and slide with prickers and chains

30th Lancers (Gordon's Horse) —*Uniform* rifle green ; *facings* white.   *Badges and De vices* — *On buttons* — Gilt raised crossed lances with pennons; ' XXX" over crossing     *On forage cap and field cap.*—In silver as on buttons.   *On pouch* —In gilt raised crossed lances with pennons;   XXX " over crossing encircled by oakleaves ; scroll below inscribed Gordon s Horse ;" the whole surmounted by a Tudor crown

31st Duke of Connaught's Own Lancers —*Uniform* blue ; *facings* scarlet   *Badges and Devices* — *On buttons.*—In brass crossed lances with pennons, with monogram ' D C O " covering the crossing of the lances   The whole surmounted by a Tudor crown   *On forage cap* —In gold embroidery crossed lances with pennons, worked in coloured silk.  A gold embroidered " 31 ' over the crossing of the lances   *On pouch.*—In gilt, the Royal and Imperial Cypher and Tudor crown   *On pouch belt* —Silver elephant with chains

32nd Lancers —*Uniform* blue ; *facings* white.   *Badges and Devices*—*On buttons* —In brass crossed lances with pennons cutting through ' 32" at point of crossing ; Tudor crown above   *On forage cap* —In gilt as on buttons. *On pouch.*—In gilt, the Royal and Imperial Cypher and Tudor crown   *On  pouch  belt* —Silver buckles, tips, slides, prickers and chains

33rd Queen Victoria s Own Light Cavalry.—*Uniform* blue ;  *facings* scarlet   *Badges and Devices.*—*On waist plate* —In silver the Royal and Imperial Cypher of Queen Victoria within the Garter surmounted by a Tudor crown and encircled with oak leaves   *On forage cap* —In brass, crossed swords with ' 33" over the crossing   Below a scroll inscribed ' Queen's Own Light Cavalry     *On pouch* —The Royal and Imperial Cypher of Queen Victoria within the Garter and Tudor crown.

34th Prince Albert Victor's Own Poona Horse —*Uniform* dark blue ;  *facings* French grey   *Badges and Devices* —*On waist plate* —In silver  the Royal and Imperial Cypher surmounted by a Tudor crown, and encircled with oak leaves   *On forage cap* —In silver gilt the monogram " P H ' *On pouch* —As on waist plate  but surrounded by a scroll inscribed with the honorary distinctions of the regiment

**35th Scinde Horse** —*Uniform* blue ; *facings* white    *Badges and Devices* —*On waist plate.*—In silver, the Royal and Imperial Cypher, surmounted by a Tudor crown, and en circled with oak leaves.    *On field cap* —The letters " S H " surrounded by a laurel wreath and surmounted by a Tudor crown    *On pouch* —The Royal and Imperial Cypher, surmount ed by a Tudor crown    *On pouch belt.*—Monogram " S H " surrounded by a laurel wreath and surmounted by a Tudor crown    Chain and whistle

**36th Jacob's Horse** —*Uniform* blue ; *facings* primrose    *Badges and Devices* —*On waist plate* —In silver    the Royal and Imperial Cypher and Tudor crown    *On forage cap.*— In silver, a device of a native horseman bearing a lance.  Below, in silver ' XXXVI Jacob's Horse.'    *On pouch* —As on waist plate    *On pouch belt* —The monogram " J H " within a laurel wreath surmounted by a Tudor crown    The whole in silver

**37th Lancers (Baluch Horse)** —*Uniform* dark blue (khaki serge when on parade with their men) ; *facings* buff    *Badges and Devices.*—*On forage cap* — Embroidered crossed lances and pennons with " 37 " over the crossing    *On field cap.*—As on forage cap.    *On pouch* —British officers --In gilt the Royal and Imperial Cypher surmounted by a Tudor crown    Indian officers —In silver, as on forage cap    *On pouch belt.*—Whistle and chain

**38th King George's Own Central India Horse.**— *Uniform* drab ; *facings* maroon. *Badges and Devices.*—*On buttons* —In gilt crossed lances bearing pennons surmounted by the monogram ' C I H.'; above a Tudor crown.    *On helmet.*—Plume of the Prince of Wales.    *On waist plate* —In silver on a gilt frosted plate the Prince of Wales's plume over crossed lances bearing pennons with " C I H ' inscribed beneath.    *On forage cap* — Crossed lances bearing pennons surmounted by the Royal and Imperial Cypher ; above, an Imperial crown ; below a scroll inscribed ' Central India Horse "    *On pouch* —Design as for forage cap    *On pouch belt* —The Prince of Wales' plume and silver prickers

**39th King George's Own Central India Horse** —*Uniform* drab ; *jacings* maroon    *Badges and Devices.*—*On buttons* —Crossed lances bearing pennons surmounted by the monogram ' C I H '; above an Imperial crown    *On shoulder* —Metal plume    *On helmet and forage cap* —Crossed lances bearing pennons surmounted by the Royal and Imperial Cypher ; above, an Imperial crown ; below a scroll inscribed    Central India Horse "    *On pouch* —As for helmet    *On pouch belt* —Plume above ' Central India Horse " between lances

**Queen Victoria's Own Corps of Guides (Lumsden's)** —*Uniform* drab ; *facings* red velvet. *Badges and Devices* —*On waist plate* —Regimental monogram surmounted by  Guides " *On field cap* —" Guides " in silver    *On pouch* —British officers —The Cypher of Queen Victoria within a Garter inscribed *Honi soit qui mal y pense*, and surmounted by a Tudor crown    The whole surrounded by a scroll bearing the words   Queen s Own Corps of Guides " Indian officers Infantry —As for British officers but smaller    Indian officers, Cavalry —The Cypher of Queen Victoria in a circle inscribed *Honi soit qui mal y pense*, and surmounted by a Tudor crown ; above the crown the word    Guides "    *On pouch belt* — Silver chains side prickers and sheath

**Aden troop** —*Uniform* khaki —*On pouch belt* —Whistle and chain.

**Indian Mountain Batteries and Frontier Garrison Artillery** —British officers as in Dress Regulations for the Army    *Badges and Devices* —Indian officers —*On buttons* — In gilt gun and Tudor crown

**1st King George's Own Sappers and Miners** —*Uniform* scarlet ; *facings* blue    *Badges and Devices. On buttons* (*Indian officers*) —In the centre the Prince of Wales' plume encircled by the words " First Sappers and Miners    *On waist plate* —In the centre the Royal and Imperial Cypher surmounted by a Tudor Crown ; underneath a scroll with the words "First King George's Own Sappers and Miners    *On helmet* (*British Non Commis sioned officers*) *and pagri* (*Indian ranks*).—The plume of the Prince of Wales,    Officers silver feathers gilt coronet    Non Commissioned officers and Indian ranks feathers white metal, coronet gilt,    *On pouch* —In the centre the Royal and Imperial Cypher surmounted by a Tudor crown ; on either side scrolls with battle honours of the corps    *On pouch belt* — Gilt engraved buckle tip and slide    In the centre of tip the letters ' S and M '

**2nd Queen Victoria's Own Sappers and Miners** —*Uniform* scarlet ; *facings* blue    *Badges and Devices* —Indian officers only    *On buttons and waist plate* —The Cypher of Queen Victoria inside the Garter, inscribed outside    Queen's Own Sappers and Miners. "    *On collar of tunic.* —A silver grenade    *On pagri* —As on buttons    *On forage cap* —[15th (Burma) Co. only] Grenade with    Burma Company    on a scroll below    *On pouch belt* —Ornamented piece of brass with ' 2nd Queen's Own Sappers and Miners ' engraved on it

**3rd Sappers and Miners** —*Uniform* scarlet ; *facings* blue    Indian officers only    *Badges and Devices* — *On buttons.*—A Tudor crown in the centre with ' 3rd Sappers and Miners ' inscribed above    *On collar of tunic and field cap* —A grenade    *On waist plate* — " E R " within a circle inscribed  ' Royal Engineers "    The whole surrounded by a laurel wreath and surmounted by a Tudor crown    *On pouch and pouch belt* —In gilt metal, the Royal Coat of Arms with scrolls below inscribed    *Ubique*    and    *Quo fas et gloria ducunt.'*

**1st Brahmans.**— *Uniform* scarlet ; *facings* white    *Badges and Devices* —On buttons ' 1 surrounded by a laurel wreath ; above a Tudor crown    *On collar of tunic and on forage cap* —Two upright fishes face to face mouths and tails touching, standing on a rectangular tablet inscribed 1776 the whole in silver gilt $1\frac{3}{4}$ inch in height

**2nd Queen Victoria's Own Rajput Light Infantry**—*Uniform* scarlet; *facings* blue. *Badges and Devices.*—*On buttons* — ' 2 " with a Tudor crown above; the whole surrounded by a laurel wreath *On collar of tunic and on helmet* (*pagri for Indian officers*)—In brass gilt, the Royal and Imperial Cypher of Queen Victoria within the Garter *On forage cap and field cap* — In silver, a bugle with   2 '   between the strings

**3rd Brahmans**—*Uniform* scarlet; *facings* black   *Badges and Devices*—*On buttons* — ": 3 " with a Tudor crown above; the whole surrounded by a laurel wreath   *On collar of tunic. helmet, forage cap and field cap* —In brass " 3 " supporting a scroll inscribed " Brahmans " and surrounded by a laurel wreath.   Above, a Tudor crown; beneath two scrolls inscribed ' Bhurtpore " ' Afghanistan 1879 80 "

**4th Prince Albert Victor's Rajputs**—*Uniform* scarlet; *facings* black   *Badges and Devices.*—*On buttons*   4 ' encircled by   Prince Albert Victor's " and below a scroll inscribed " Rajputs "   The whole surmounted by a Tudor crown   *On field cap*   " IV " surmounted by a Tudor crown with   Rajputs ' on a scroll below

**5th Light Infantry**—*Uniform* scarlet; *facings* yellow.   *Badges and Devices*—*On buttons*—A bugle with   5 ' between the strings; below, ' Light Infantry "; above a Tudor crown.   *On helmet*—In gilt a bugle and strings with "5 below   *On forage cap.*—In gilt a bugle with ' V" between the strings   *On field cap*—As on forage cap embroidered in gold

**6th Jat Light Infantry**—*Uniform* scarlet; *facings* white   *Badges and Devices.*—*On buttons*—A bugle with ' 6   between the strings; above a Tudor crown   *On collar of tunic*—A gold embroidered bugle with strings   *On helmet.*—Brass bugle and strings with " 6 ' below   *On field cap*—As on collar of tunic with   6 ' below

**7th Duke of Connaught's Own Rajputs**—*Uniform* scarlet; *facings* yellow.   *Badges and Devices*—The crest of His Royal Highness the Duke of Connaught   Beneath it and round the rim ' D. C O Rajputs"   *On collar of tunic*—In silver the Crest and Cypher of His Royal Highness the Duke of Connaught surrounded by laurel leaves unfolded in a scroll bearing the words   Duke of Connaught's Own " and ' VII "   *On helmet* (*pagri Indian officers*)— As on collar of tunic but in gilt   *On forage cap and field cap and lapel of mess jacket*—As on collar of tunic in silver but reduced in size and the laurel leaves and scroll are omitted

**8th Rajputs**—*Uniform* scarlet; *facings* yellow   *Badges and Devices*—*On buttons.*—" VIII   with a Tudor crown above; the whole encircled by a band inscribed ' Rajputs in upper half   and ' Sobraon " in lower   *On pagris* (*Indian officers*).—In silver  ' 8 encircled by a band inscribed   Rajputs " above, with two laurel branches tied below   Above a Tudor crown; the whole encircled by a laurel wreath   *On field cap*—In brass ' VIII ' surmounted by a Tudor crown; below, a scroll inscribed ' Rajputs '

**9th Bhopal Infantry**—*Uniform* drab; *facings* chocolate   *Badges and Devices*—*On buttons*—A bugle with   9 ' interwoven   *On collar of tunic*—A silver fish   *On field cap* — In silver, as on buttons

**10th Jats**—*Uniform* scarlet; *facings* yellow   *Badges and Devices.*—*On buttons.*—" X " with a Tudor crown above and ' Jats" below   The whole surrounded by a laurel wreath. *On helmet and field cap*—' X ' with a Tudor crown above and scroll below inscribed ' Jats "

**11th Rajputs**—*Uniform* scarlet; *facings* yellow   *Badges and Devices.*—*On buttons* — ' XI " encircled by a band inscribed   Rajputs " with a Tudor crown above; the whole surrounded by a laurel wreath   *On field cap* — ' XI "

**12th Pioneers (Kelat i Ghilzai Regiment)**—*Uniform* scarlet; *facings* black.—*Badges and Devices*—*On buttons*—  XII ' with a mural crown above; the whole enclosed within a band inscribed ' Kelat i Ghilzai'   Pioneers"   *On helmet*—A six pointed star on a brass plate with ' 12 ' inside a band inscribed ' Kelat i Ghilzai Regiment"; above the circle a mural crown; below the circle, two axes crossed   *On forage cap and field cap*—In silver "XII' surmounted by a mural crown; below two axes crossed

**13th Rajputs (The Shekhawati Regiment)**—*Uniform* scarlet; *facings* blue   *Badges and Devices*—*On buttons*— '13" encircled by a band inscribed   The Shekhawati Regiment"; above, a Tudor crown, the whole surrounded by a laurel wreath and resting on a scroll inscribed ' Rajputs.'   *On helmet forage cap, field cap   roll collar* (*mess dress*)   *collar serge jacket* (*drill order*) *and collar of white frock and tunic*—In silver two Rajput daggers crossed, points upwards, between the handles   13 ' in silver gilt

**14th King George's Own Ferozepore Sikhs**—*Uniform* scarlet; *facings* yellow   *Badges and Devices* — *On buttons.*— K. G. O   Sikhs" on an embossed Quoit   "14" in centre of Quoit   *On collar of tunic*—The Royal and Imperial Cypher surmounted by a Tudor crown.   *On helmet*—Silver Quoit; Prince of Wales's plume superimposed   *On forage and field cap*—Small silver Quoit surmounted by Prince of Wales' plume   *On mess jacket*—Silver Quoit surmounted by the Royal and Imperial Cypher and Tudor crown

**15th Ludhiana Sikhs.**—*Uniform* scarlet; *facings* emerald green.   *Badges and Devices.*—*On buttons* — 15' within a quoit inscribed   Ludhiana Sikhs" and surmounted by a Tudor crown   *On collar of tunic* —(British officers) a small silver quoit   *On helmet*—A silver quoit with   XV ' in centre; ' Ludhiana Sikhs " on a scroll below   The whole surmounted by a Tudor crown   *On forage cap*—A plain silver quoit

**16th Rajputs (The Lucknow Regiment)**—*Uniform* scarlet; *facings* white.   *Badges and Devices*—*On buttons*—"16' in centre with   Lucknow Regiment ' round it   *On*

*collar of tunic* and *mess jacket* —(British officers) A turreted gateway  *On helmet.*—(Pagri Indian officers )  A turreted gateway; above, "16 ' —*On field cap.*—A turreted gateway.

**17th Infantry (The Loyal Regiment)** —*Uniform* scarlet ; *facings* white  *Badges and Devices* —*On buttons* —' XVII" encircled by a band inscribed " The Loyal Regiment," above a Tudor crown ; on outer circle eight laurel leaves with stems.  *On collar of tunic and on field cap* —A silver crescent  *On helmet* —In silver  "XVII" within a silver crescent ; above, a Tudor crown

**18th Infantry** —*Uniform* scarlet ; *facings* black.  *Badges and Devices* —*On buttons.*— "18' encircled by a band charged with the word "Infantry" and two laurel branches; above a Tudor crown ; the whole encircled by a laurel wreath  *On collar of tunic, helmet, forage cap and field cap* —Crescent and star in silver plated metal

**19th Punjabis** —*Uniform* scarlet ; *facings* dark blue.- *Badges and Devices* —*On buttons* - "XIX" surmounted by a Tudor crown and ' Punjabis " on a plain circle round the edge.  *On field cap* —  XIX " surmounted by a Tudor crown  Below a scroll inscribed " Punjabis."

**20th Duke of Cambridge's Own Infantry (Brownlow's Punjabis)** —*Uniform* drab, *facings* emerald green  *Badges and Devices* —*On buttons* —In silver a Maltese cross with "XX" surrounded by ' D. C O Infantry ' in centre  *On field cap* —A silver bugle  *On pouch* —A wreath intertwined with a scroll inscribed, "Pekin, ' " Taku Forts,  'Afghanistan 1878 80, ' ' Ali Musjid " on the left, and ' Egypt, 1882," " Tel el Kebir  ' Punjab Frontier'  China, 1900, on the right.  Surmounted by a Tudor crown, and below on a scroll, " Duke of Cambridge's Own "  In the centre two G's locked into one another  *On pouch belt.* —In silver a Maltese cross, containing on its centre, which is domed and of polished silver, the number ' XX'  A circlet surrounds this dome, and is inscribed ' D C O  Infantry '  The surface of this circlet and of the cross is of chased silver. A laurel wreath surrounds the cross with scrolls inscribed " Taku Forts ' " Ali Musjid," " Egypt, 1882 " and ' Punjab Frontier  on the left, and ' Pekin," " Afghanistan, 1878 80, " Tel el Kebir  " China, 1900 " on the right.  The wreath surmounted by a Tudor crown  " Brownlow s Punjabis " on a scroll attached to and below the wreath.

**21st Punjabis.** —*Uniform* drab ; *facings* scarlet.—*Badges and Devices* —*On helmet and field cap* — Silver circle inscribed " Punjabis" with "XXI ' in centre surmounted by a Tudor crown  *On waist plate* —(Indian officers)—" XXI " surrounded by ' Punjabis ' The whole encircled by a laurel wreath and surmounted by a Tudor crown  *On pouch* —As on waist plate  *On pouch belt* - A six pointed silver star on silver plaque with raised circle in centre inscribed  Punjabis.'  XXI ' in centre  The whole surrounded by a laurel wreath and surmounted by a Tudor crown  Above a silver ribbon inscribed " Abyssinia ; below another inscribed ' Afghanistan, 1878 80 "  Above the upper ribbon, a lion s head holding the whistle chain.  Below the lower ribbon, a silver whistle in a silver octagonal sheath, with ornamentation of acorns and oak leaves.

**22nd Punjabis** —*Uniform* scarlet ; *facings* blue  *Badges and Devices.*—*On buttons* — "22" surmounted by a Tudor crown and encircled by a laurel wreath ;  Punjabis " on the upper edge.  *On helmet* —'22' inside a plain brass circle.  Punjabis ' on upper half of circle  Encircled by a laurel wreath, surmounted by a Tudor crown  *On field cap* — ' XXII " with scroll below inscribed " Punjabis "; the whole surmounted by a Tudor crown

**23rd Sikh Pioneers** —*Uniform* drab; *facings* chocolate  *Badges and Devices* —*On forage cap* —In silver, a Sikh quoit on a piece of chocolate cloth, inscribed ' Sikh' supporting a Tudor crown and resting on a scroll inscribed " Pioneers '.  " XXIII " in centre of quoit.  *On pouch* — '23 " on dark chocolate ground surrounded by an oval silver circle inscribed " Sikh Pioneers " surrounded by a laurel, round and about which winds a silver scroll bearing the distinctions of the regiment.  *On pouch belt* —A silver Maltese cross on a burnished silver plate surmounted by a Tudor crown  In the centre of the cross " 23 " on a dark chocolate ground surrounded by a circle inscribed ' Sikh Pioneers "  Between each of the arms of the cross, a silver lion rampant  On the arms of the cross, the distinctions of the regiment.

**24th Punjabis.** —*Uniform* scarlet ; *facings* white  *Badges and Devices* —*On buttons.*— ' 24 " surmounted by a Tudor crown.  *On forage cap* —In silver, a five pointed star with small ball at each re entrant  A circle inside star inscribed  Punjabis ' on top and laurel leaves underneath ; " 24 " inside circle on frosted ground  Above star a Tudor crown in silver

**25th Punjabis** —*Uniform* scarlet ; *facings* white  *Badges and Devices* —*On buttons* — "25 ' in centre and  Punjabis' inscribed on a band round the edge.  *On helmet and forage cap.* —In gold (silver on forage cap) ' XXV ' in centre surrounded by a gold circle inscribed " Punjabis "  The whole surrounded by a laurel wreath and surmounted by a Tudor crown

**26th Punjabis.** —*Uniform* drab ; *facings* scarlet  *Badges and Devices* —*On field cap.*— A silver bugle. *On pouch* —' 26 " in two concentric circles inscribed ' Punjabis,' encircled by branches of bay leaves  *On pouch belt* —In silver, a Maltese cross, the eight extreme ends of which end in balls  Between each of the arms a lion rampant facing inwards.  In the centre of the cross " 26 ' on a convex ground surrounded by the word " Punjabis ' within two concentric circles  The whole encircled by 2 branches of bay leaves secured by a knot at the junction, and surmounted by Tudor crown  *On forage cap* —As on pouch belt, in white metal

**27th Punjabis**—*Uniform* drab; *facings* scarlet   *Badges and Devices,—On buttons.*—" XXVII ' above " Punjabis '   *On forage cap*—The Royal and Imperial Cypher within the Garter inscribed *Honi soit qui mal y pense.*   A Tudor crown above the whole encircled by a laurel wreath   Below, a scroll inscribed " XXVII Punjabis '   *On pouch.*—As on forage cap.   *On pouch belt*—As on pouch, but with a scroll inscribed " China, 1860 62 " between the Crown and the Garter

**28th Punjabis**—*Uniform* scarlet; *facings* emerald green   *Badges and Devices*—*On buttons*—A quoit inscribed " Punjabis ' on lower half; above, a Tudor crown; in centre " 28 "; the whole encircled by a laurel wreath   *On helmet*—In silver  a Sikh quoit with frosted crescent interlaced; on the crescent " 28 '; above a Tudor crown   *On forage cap and field cap.*—A gilt quoit with frosted crescent interlaced   On the crescent " 28 " in raised figures; above a Tudor crown

**29th Punjabis**—*Uniform* scarlet; *facings* blue.   *Badges and Devices.—On buttons*—" 29 "   *On field cap*—" 29 " surmounted by a Tudor crown with scroll below inscribed " Punjabis "

**30th Punjabis**—*Uniform* scarlet; *facings* white.   *Badges and Devices*—*On buttons*—(Mess waistcoat only) " 30 ' surmounted by a Tudor crown   Below a scroll inscribed " Punjabis."   *On helmet and forage cap*—A quoit in plain lines with " XXX " in centre surmounted by a Tudor crown and encircled by laurels; scroll below inscribed " Punjabis "   *On field cap*—' XXX " surmounted by a Tudor crown, with a scroll below, inscribed " Punjabis "

**31st Punjabis**—*Uniform* scarlet; *facings* white   *Badges and Devices*—*On buttons*—" 31 " surmounted by a Tudor crown with " Punjabis " in lower portion of outer circle   *On helmet, forage cap and field cap*—In silver a Maltese cross surmounted by a Tudor crown with " 31 ' in centre circle of cross and four lions between the arms of the cross

**32nd Sikh Pioneers**—*Uniform* scarlet; *facings* dark blue   *Badges and Devices.—On buttons*—A Tudor crown supported by two felling axes crossed; " XXXII " below   *On collar of tunic and mess jacket*—(Indian officers—on collar of tunic Hot Weather and Service Dress)—Crossed silver axes.   *On helmet.*—(*Pagri, Indian officers*) *and on field cap*—A Sikh quoit inscribed   XXXII Sikh Pioneers" bearing at the foot, on a scroll, the motto *Aut viam inveniam aut faciam*   The whole surmounted by a Tudor crown supported by two felling axes crossed

**33rd Punjabis**—*Uniform* drab; *facings* green   *Badges and Devices*—*On field cap*—A crescent with five pointed star; on the star   33 '   The whole surrounded by a laurel wreath and scroll inscribed   Punjabis;" a Tudor crown above   *On pouch.*—" 33   surrounded by a band inscribed " Punjabis   the whole encircled by a laurel wreath; above, a Tudor crown   *On pouch belt*—On a plain silver plate a Maltese cross the points of which end in balls; between the arms four lions rampant facing inwards   In the centre of the cross on a convex ground ' 33 " surrounded by a band inscribed " Punjabis '   The whole encircled by a laurel wreath   Above, a Tudor crown

**34th Sikh Pioneers**—*Uniform* scarlet; *facings* dark blue.   *Badges and Devices.—On buttons*—  34 " enclosed in  a quoit inscribed ' Sikh Pioneers " surmounted by a Tudor crown   *On collar of tunic*  (H W. and S. D uniform )—In silver, crossed axes (Indian officers—in German silver.)—*On helmet.*—(*Pagri  Indian officers*)—Gilt star with a quoit inscribed ' Sikh Pioneers" surmounted by a Tudor crown  and silver crossed axes below   " 34" on a blue ground in centre of quoit   *On forage cap*—Crossed axes surmounted by a quoit enclosing " 34"; the whole surmounted by a Tudor crown

**35th Sikhs**—*Uniform* scarlet; *facings* yellow   *Badges and Devices*—*On buttons.*—" 35 " within a quoit inscribed " Sikhs,' surmounted by a Tudor crown.   *On collar of tunic, khaki and white jacket and mess jacket*—A small silver quoit   *On helmet*—A silver quoit surmounted by a Tudor crown and inscribed ' Sikhs" on lower half and ' XXXV" across the middle, on a yellow silk background   *On forage cap and field cap.*—A silver quoit inscribed " XXXV ' and  Sikhs " on the upper and lower halves respectively

**36th Sikhs**—*Uniform* scarlet; *facings* yellow   *Badges and Devices*—*On buttons helmet* (*Indian Officers—on pagri*) *and  forage cap.*—Crossed quoits surmounted by a Tudor crown and surrounded by a laurel wreath; " XXXVI Sikhs ' in centre   *On collar of tunic and khaki jacket.*—Small brass crossed quoits.

**37th Dogras**—*Uniform* scarlet; *facings* yellow.   *Badges and Devices*—*On buttons*—" 37 " surmounted by a Tudor crown; below ' Dogras '   *On field cap.*—' 37 ' surmounted by a Tudor crown; below the word " Dogras " the letters interlaced on a curve, the whole in silver

**38th Dogras**—*Uniform* scarlet; *facings* yellow   *Badges and Devices*—*On buttons, helmet, and forage cap*—' 38 " surmounted by a Tudor crown, and a scroll below inscribed " Dogras.'

**39th Garhwal Rifles.**—*Uniform* dark green; *facings* black.—*Badges and Devices*—*On buttons.*— 39 " within the strings of a bugle; above  a Tudor crown   *On helmet*—On a silver eight pointed star, a bronze Maltese cross bearing in the centre a stringed bugle within a band inscribed " Garhwal Rifles "   *On forage cap and field cap*—On a silver Maltese cross a stringed bugle within a band inscribed " Garhwal Rifles "   *On pouch.*—A silver bugle stringed; below a scroll inscribed " Garhwal Rifles '   *On pouch belt*—A silver Maltese cross encircled by an oak  wreath; in centre, a bugle stringed within a band inscribed " Garhwal Rifles '; above, a Tudor crown

**40th Pathans** —*Uniform* drab ; *facings* emerald green. *Badges and Devices* —*On forage cap.*—In silver, two Pathan knives crossed behind a round shield. " 40 " attached to top of shield between the blades of the knives. "Pathans" on a scroll below the shield, the ends of the scroll being joined to the handles of the knives   *On pouch.*—In silver " 40 " within a band inscribed " Pathans   The whole surrounded by a laurel wreath ; above, a Tudor crown   *On pouch belt*—A plain silver plate on which is a laurel wreath surmounted by a Tudor crown.   Inside the wreath a Maltese cross having " 40 ' in the centre surrounded by a circlet inscribed ' Pathans "

**41st Dogras** —*Uniform* scarlet ; *facings* yellow   *Badges and Devices* —*On buttons* (except mess waistcoat) —' 41 " surmounted by a Tudor crown and ' Dogras   below.   *On helmet   forage cap, field cap and mess waistcoat buttons* —As on buttons, except that " Dogras ' is on a scroll

**42nd Deoli Regiment** —*Uniform* dark green ; *facings* scarlet   *Badges and Devices.* *On buttons* (bronze) —' 42 "   *On forage cap and pouch and pouch belt.*—An oval with the motto   *E turba legio* encircling a six pointed star in the centre of which is a shield bearing " XLII "   The whole surmounted by a turret

**43rd Erinpura Regiment.**—*Uniform* dark green ; *facings* scarlet   *Badges and Devices* — *On buttons* (gilt)   ' 43 " with a shamrock wreath   *On helmet   pouch and forage cap* —A crossed Hindu dagger and Muhammadan knife over ' 43 '

**44th Merwara Infantry** —*Uniform* scarlet ; *facings* gosling green   *Badges and Devices* — *On buttons* —A Mer tower   *On collar of tunic and mess jacket and on helmet* —A silver tower   *On field cap* —A tower, one inch high, worked in gold thread on a black ground

**45th Rattray's Sikhs** —*Uniform* scarlet ; *facings* white   *Badges and Devices* —*On buttons* —A Sikh quoit inscribed   Rattray s Sikhs   " 45   in centre   The whole surmounted by a Tudor crown   *On helmet and field cap.*—A Sikh quoit surmounted by a dagger.

**46th Punjabis** —*Uniform* drab ; *facings* emerald green   *Badges and Devices* —*On pouch belt* —A convex circular shield on which is a raised quoit with two Pathan knives crossing inside it, and the figure   46 "   Above the shield a Tudor crown ; below the quoit, and touching the handles of the Pathan knives a crescent inscribed " Punjabis '   The whole shield surrounded by a laurel wreath, the extreme points meeting at the base of the Tudor crown   *On pouch* —As above but omitting the shield

**47th Sikhs** — *Uniform* scarlet ; *facings* yellow   *Badges and Devices* —*On buttons* — Quoit surmounted by a Tudor crown ; ' XLVII   across centre, and ' Sikhs " on lower face of quoit   Rim round edge of button   *On collar of tunic.*—Silver quoit. *On helmet* —Silver quoit with   XLVII   Sikhs " across centre   Yellow cloth under centre. *On forage cap and field cap.*—Silver quoit surmounted by a Tudor crown ; " XLVII " across centre

**48th Pioneers** —*Uniform* scarlet ; *facings* black —*Badges and Devices* —*On buttons* — Two axes crossed ;   48 " above ; the whole surmounted by a Tudor crown   *On collar of tunic, mess jacket, H W and S D uniform* —In silver, two axes crossed.   *On helmet and field cap* —In silver a six pointed star charged with two axes crossed in gilt   (Indian officers, on pagri, a similar badge but larger )

**51st Sikhs (Frontier Force)** —*Uniform* drab ; *facings* yellow   *Badges and Devices* —*On buttons* —A Sikh quoit, inscribed ' Sikhs F F ' with ' 51 ' in centre   *On waist plate and pouch belt* —Burnished silver quoit surmounted by a Tudor crown and inscribed " Sikhs " on upper part of quoit, with ' 51   in raised burnished silver on a boss of frosted silver   A scroll with ' Frontier Force ' as a base and   Afghanistan, 1878 79 " and ' Ali Musjid " on right of quoit and ' Punjab " and " Pekin 1900 " on left   The quoit is encircled by a laurel wreath   *On field cap and pouch* —As on waist plate, but without the honorary distinctions.

**52nd Sikhs (Frontier Force)** —*Uniform* drab ; *facings* scarlet   *Badges and Devices.* *Buttons* —Are of silver, hemispherical (diameter   65 inch)   *On waist plate* —(Indian Officers). A bugle surmounted by a Tudor crown ; a scroll across the bugle inscribed ' Sikhs, F F ' and below ' 52 " *On field cap.*—As on Indian officers' waist plate   *On pouch and pouch belt* —' 52 ' on a silver boss within a quoit encircled by a laurel wreath ; the whole surmounted by a Tudor crown.   On scrolls on the branches of the wreath   Punjab " and   Kandahar   1880 " on the left " Ahmed Khel   and ' Afghanistan 1878 80 " on the right.   Below, a scroll inscribed ' Sikhs Frontier Force ' round lower half of quoit

**53rd Sikhs (Frontier Force)** —*Uniform* drab ; *facings* bulek   *Badges and Devices* —*On buttons.*—The Royal and Imperial Cypher surmounted by a Tudor crown   *On forage cap* — A Sikh lion   surmounted by a Tudor crown   astride over " 53,' below a scroll inscribed " Sikhs "   *On pouch* —A Sikh lion rampant within a quoit inscribed " 53 Sikhs " and surrounded by a laurel wreath on which are two scrolls inscribed   Afghanistan 1879 80 " ' Kabul, 1879,' ' Kandahar 1880 " and   Punjab Frontier ' respectively   Over base of wreath a small scroll inscribed   Tirah " and below a larger scroll inscribed " Frontier Force '   The whole surmounted by a Tudor crown   *On pouch belt* —An eight pointed star In centre   ' 53 " surmounted by a Tudor crown and surrounded by a laurel wreath which is crossed at base by a scroll inscribed ' Tirah " Surrounding the laurel wreath are three scrolls, two on either side above inscribed   Kabul, 1879 " and   Kandahar 1880   respectively and one below inscribed ' Sikhs   Frontier Force   Below, a double scroll inscribed Afghanistan, 1879 80 " and " Punjab Frontier "

**54th Sikhs (Frontier Force)** —*Uniform* drab ; *facings* emerald green    *Badges and Devices* —*On forage cap, field cap, pouch and pouch belt*.—A laurel wreath surmounted by a Tudor crown    Within the wreath a circle inscribed " Sikhs, Frontier Force," " 54 ' within the circle, below which is a bugle    Below the wreath a scroll inscribed " Pegu,' " Delhi," ' Chitral."

**55th Coke's Rifles (Frontier Force)** —*Uniform* dark green ; *facings* scarlet (piping)    *Badges and Devices* —*On buttons* —A bugle of special pattern.    *On helmet* —A silver bugle with ' 55 ' in centre and scroll inscribed " Delhi ", " Afghanistan, 1878—79 '    *On forage cap, field cap and pouch* —A silver bugle    *On pouch belt* —A Maltese cross with bugle and " 55 " in centre, with scrolls as on helmet badge    Boss a lion's head, inscribed " Coke's Rifles, Frontier Force "

**56th Punjabi Rifles (Frontier Force)** —*Uniform* drab ; *facings* black    *Badges and Devices* —*On field cap* —In silver, a stringed bugle crossed by a scroll inscribed " 56th Punjabi Rifles."    *On pouch and pouch belt* —' 56 " in plain relief on a circular plain silver shield surrounded by ' Punjabi Rifles (Frontier Force) " inscribed in a rough circular band surmounted by a Tudor crown.    Branches of rose shamrock and thistle either side.    Scroll intertwined, inscribed ' Delhi,'    Lucknow    Peiwar Kotal '    " Afghanistan 1878—79 " " Punjab Frontier', ' Tirah ' in plain relief

**57th Wilde's Rifles (Frontier Force)** —*Uniform* drab ; *facings* blue.    *Badges and Devices.*—*On forage cap* —In silver ' 57 " within a circle inscribed " Wilde's Rifles ' and surmounted by a Tudor crown    *On pouch* — 57 " on a silver boss within a circle inscribed ' Wilde's Rifles '    Laurel leaves round the sides and bottom of the circle    On a ribbon on the laurel leaves,    Delhi "    ' Lucknow,'    " Afghanistan, 1879—80," " China 1900 ' from left to right    Below    another ribbon inscribed " Frontier Force "    The whole surmounted by a Tudor crown    *On pouch belt* —As on pouch    The honorary distinctions " Delhi ' and    Afghanistan 1878 79 " are on ribbons on either side of the circle, and " Lucknow ' and " China 1900 " on two ribbons below it

**58th Vaughan's Rifles (Frontier Force).** —*Uniform* drab ; *facings* emerald green.    *Badges and Devices.*—*On helmet, field cap and forage cap* —A quoit inscribed " Vaughan's Rifles " with a silver plate containing " 58 ' in centre and surmounted by a Tudor crown ; under the quoit, and attached to it, a scroll inscribed ' Frontier Force "    *On pouch and pouch belt*— 58 " on a silver plate forming the centre of a quoit on which is inscribed ' Vaughan's Rifles "    The quoit encircled by laurel wreaths bearing the honorary distinction of the regiment and surmounted by a Tudor crown    A scroll below the wreaths inscribed    Frontier Force "

**59th Scinde Rifles (Frontier Force)** —*Uniform* drab ; *facings* scarlet.    *Badges and Devices.*—*On buttons* —Bugle surmounted by a Tudor crown    *On helmet.*—A Maltese cross in black metal with a lion between each arm of the cross ; in the centre " 59 ' on a blue ground, in a circle inscribed    Scinde Rifles    Frontier Force '    *On field cap* —In silver, as on helmet, but with a scroll below, inscribed " Ready, aye ready '    *On pouch* —In silver a bugle with " 59 ' in centre, and ' Ready, aye ready ' on a scroll below    *On pouch belt* —In silver, as on helmet embossed lion's head (for whistle and chain) with motto " Ready, aye ready " surrounding it

**61st King George's Own Pioneers** —*Uniform* scarlet ; *facings* white.    *Badges and Devices* —*On buttons* —A circular band surmounted by a Tudor crown with ' 61" within and " Pioneers ' and ' Seetabuldee ' inscribed on the band    The whole encircled by laurel wreaths with    1758 ' on a scroll binding them together.    *On collar* (all garments)— Crossed pick and shovel in brass surmounted by the Prince of Wales' plume    coronet and motto in white metal    *On helmet* —In polished brass    The Garter with the motto ' Honi soit qui mal y pense" inserted thereon and    the Royal and Imperial Cypher surmounted by a crown inserted in the centre    The whole encircled by laurel wreaths, surmounted by the Prince of Wales' plume    A scroll beneath inscribed " 61st K G O    Pioneers "    *On forage and field cap* —In polished brass.    Pierced circle with " Pioneers " in upper half and " 1758 " in lower half and within the circle ' LXI ' in brass    The whole surmounted by the Prince of Wales's plume    Coronet and motto in white metal    Under the whole a scroll in white metal containing the words " King George's Own "

**62nd Punjabis** —*Uniform* scarlet ; *facings* green.    *Badges and Devices* —*On buttons.*— Within a waved border, an elephant; below, and at the sides of the elephant, scrolls inscribed ' China" ' Assaye "    ' Nagpore "    Beneath the golden dragon wearing an Imperial crown    The whole in brass    *On collar of tunic and lapel of mess jacket.*—The elephant in silver, preceding the golden dragon wearing an Imperial crown    The whole surmounted by a Tudor crown.    The whole in silver    *On helmet* —A Sikh quoit gold and red    Within the quoit an elephant, gold.    Below the quoit a green enamelled scroll inscribed in gilt lettering    62nd Punjabis '    Below the scroll, the golden dragon wearing an Imperial crown    *On forage and field cap.*—As on helmet.

**63rd Palamcottah Light Infantry** —*Uniform* scarlet ; *facings* emerald green    *Badge and Devices* —*On buttons* —    63 " within a circle inscribed 'Now or never," encircled by a wreath ; the whole surmounted by a Tudor crown.    *On collar of tunic    khaki jacket, and helmet* (Indian officers—pagri), *forage cap, field cap* —A bugle surmounted by Tudor crown with " 63 " between the strings

**64th Pioneers** —*Uniform* scarlet ; *facings* white.    *Badges and Devices* —*On buttons.*— " 64    surmounted by an elephant and crossed felling axes with    Pioneers ' inscribed *underneath. On collar of tunic and field cap*—Crossed felling axes   *On helmet.*—Oval shaped badge with ' 64 ' in centre ' Pioneers ' at bottom ; surmounted by the elephant standing on top of the oval with " Assaye " underneath.

**66th Punjabis.**—*Uniform* scarlet ; *facings* green.   *Badges and Devices—On buttons*— " 66 " within a circle inscribed the word " Punjabis ' at the top and a spray of laurel underneath a narrow rim at the edge   *Mess Waistcoat buttons.*—Small brass button surmounted by a small golden dragon   *On collar of tunic*—A small golden dragon wearing an Imperial crown   *On forage and field cap*—A small golden dragon wearing an Imperial crown   *On Mess jacket (worn on each lapel)*—A small golden dragon wearing an Imperial crown

**67th Punjabis.**—*Uniform* scarlet ; *facings* emerald green   *Badges and Devices.*—On *buttons* —' 67 Punjabis' surmounted by a Tudor crown   *On forage cap and field cap* —' 67 encircled by a Sikh quoit ; below a crescent inscribed Punjabis '; below the crescent, a scroll inscribed Carnatic ', ' Ava ' Mysore '   Above the whole a Tudor crown

**69th Punjabis** —*Uniform* scarlet ; *facings* emerald green   *Badges and Devices.*—On *buttons* —A Tudor crown with 69 ' below   (A special flat gilt button inscribed 69 in silver for mess waistcoat )   *On collar of tunic forage cap and field cap* —A galley in gold braid

**72nd Punjabis** —*Uniform* drab serge ; *facings* white   *Badges and Devices* —On but tons.—Burmese peacock in centre with " 72 " above and   Punjabis ' below   *On helmet (Indian officers—pagri*, in white metal)   *forage cap ; field cap* ; *pouch belt* —Burmese peacock.   Beneath a scroll inscribed 72nd Punjabis "   *On pouch* — ' 72 " over ' Punjabis " in circular form

**73rd Carnatic Infantry** —*Uniform* scarlet ; *facings* white   *Badges and Devices* —On *buttons* —' LXXIII " surmounted by a Tudor crown   *On helmet (Indian officers—pagri) and field cap* —' LXXIII " with   Carnatic Infantry " in the centre of a star within a scroll bearing the words Carnatic ", Sholinghur Mysore' Seringapatam " ' Burma, 1885 87 '   The whole surmounted by a Tudor crown.

**74th Punjabis** —*Uniform* scarlet ; *facings* emerald green   *Badges and Devices* —On *buttons*, forage cap and field cap* —" 74 " surmounted by the dragon *On collar of tunic* — The dragon —Also worn on full dress pagri and on collar of tunic by Indian officers   A similar badge but metal instead of embroidered is worn by officers on all jackets   *On helmet* —The dragon

**75th Carnatic Infantry** —*Uniform* scarlet ; *facings* yellow   *Badges and Devices.*—On *buttons.*— 75 in centre within a double circle inscribed ' Carnatic Infantry ".   *On collar of tunic ; mess jacket ; white frock ; helmet ; field cap* —In silver the Star of India with a brass scroll in centre inscribed   Carnatic Infantry   ' 75 " in brass in centre of scroll

**76th Punjabis** —*Uniform* scarlet ; *facings* emerald green.   *Badges and Devices* — *On buttons and forage cap.*— ' 76 " within a circle inscribed ' Punjabis surmounted by a Tudor crown and surrounded by a laurel wreath

**79th Carnatic Infantry.**—*Uniform* scarlet ; *facings* yellow   *Badges and Devices* —On *buttons* — ' 79 " encircled by ' Carnatic Infantry ' inside a laurel wreath and surmounted by a Tudor crown   *On collar of tunic, mess jacket and khaki jacket* - A silver elephant *On forage cap and field cap* —An elephant above ' 79 "

**80th Carnatic Infantry** —*Uniform* scarlet ; *facings* emerald green.   *Badges and Devices* —On *buttons* — 80 ' surrounded by a laurel wreath and surmounted by a Tudor crown

**81st Pioneers** —*Uniform* scarlet ; *facings* white   *Badges and Devices* —On *buttons* —A laurel wreath surmounted by a Tudor crown ; with ' 81 '' in centre   *On collar of tunic field cap* —Crossed felling axes   *On helmet (Indian officers—pagri).*—' 81 within a circle inscribed ' Pioneers   the whole surrounded by a laurel wreath and surmounted by a Tudor crown.

**82nd Punjabis** —*Uniform* scarlet ; *facings* emerald green   *Badges and Devices* —On *buttons* — 82 " surmounted by a Tudor crown   *On helmet* —An eight pointed star   A plain ' 82 on a silver back ground surmounted by a Tudor crown   A scroll below inscribed ' Punjabis."   *On forage cap* —An eight pointed silver star

**83rd Wallajahbad Light Infantry** —*Uniform* scarlet ; *facings* emerald green.   *Badges and Devices* —On *buttons.*—A bugle with ' 83 in centre surmounted by a Tudor crown and surrounded by   Wallajahbad Light Infantry '   *On collar of tunic forage cap and field cap* —A bugle with ' 83 ' in centre   *On helmet (Indian officers—pagri)* —As on collar of tunic, but with a scroll inscribed ' Now or never " below.

**84th Punjabis** —*Uniform* scarlet ; *facings* emerald green   *Badges and Devices* —On *buttons* —The elephant surmounted by a Tudor crown, encircled by the distinctions of the regiment ; underneath 84 "   *On forage cap and field cap* —A silver elephant surmounting ' 84 "

**86th Carnatic Infantry** —*Uniform* scarlet ; *facings* emerald green   *Badges and Devices* —On *buttons* — 86 within a circle surmounted by a Tudor crown and inscribed Carnatic Infantry "   *On collar of tunic and mess jacket* —As on buttons   The whole in the centre of a silver star   The 86 " is in silver the circle crown and centre background of brass   *On helmet and field cap* —As on collar of tunic but entirely of silver

**87th Punjabis** —*Uniform* scarlet ; *facings* emerald green.   *Badges and Devices.*— On *buttons* — 87 ' within two concentric circles inscribed Punjabis ' surmounted by a Tudor crown  *On helmet and forage cap* — 87   within two concentric circles inscribed "Punjabis , the whole contained within the Star of India surmounted by a Tudor crown

**88th Carnatic Infantry** —*Uniform* scarlet ; *facings* yellow. *Badges and Devices.*—*On buttons* — 88 ' surmounted by a Tudor crown  *On helmet* —British officers.—A ten pointed star of gilt metal surmounted by a Tudor crown ; on the star a silver badge consisting of ' 88 ' inside a circle inscribed ' Carnatic Infantry ' surrounded by a laurel wreath with a scroll entwined inscribed ' Mahidpore " ' Nagpore ', ' Ava " and ' China 1900 " Indian officers (on pagri) —A silver badge consisting of " 88 inside a circle inscribed ' Carnatic Infantry " partly surrounded by a laurel wreath and surmounted by a Tudor crown. *On forage cap* — 88 ' inside a circle inscribed ' Carnatic Infantry " surrounded by a laurel wreath with a scroll entwined bearing the honorary distinctions of the regiment The whole surmounted by a Tudor crown in embossed silver

**89th Punjabis** —*Uniform* drab ; *facings* blue. *Badges and Devices* —*On buttons.*— ' 89 " surmounted by a Tudor crown ; ' Punjabis " underneath and round edge of button *On helmet, field cap  and pouch belt* —A Sikh quoit and crescent ; Regimental and King's colours crossing behind the quoit and the crescent The whole surmounted by a Tudor crown ; underneath a scroll inscribed 89th Punjabis ' *On pouch* — 89 " in silver

**90th Punjabis** —*Uniform* drab ; *facings* black  *Badges and Devices* —*On but tons* — 90 ' within a scroll inscribed Punjabis" surmounted by a Tudor crown and semi enclosed by a laurel wreath  *On helmet and field cap* —A Sikh quoit surmounted by a Tudor crown and enclosing a Burmese lion ; below ' 90"; above a scroll inscribed ' Punjabis "  *On pouch* — 90 " surmounted by a Tudor crown; below, a scroll inscribed ' Punjabis.  *On pouch belt* —An eight pointed star, chased the upper points inscribed ' Ava '   Burma 1885 87 "  Below on a scroll, ' Afghanistan 1878 80 '  In the centre, below a Tudor crown, a Sikh quoit encircling a Burmese lion, and on a laurel wreath and scroll beneath, ' 90 Punjabis '

**91st Punjabis (Light Infantry)** —*Uniform* drab ; *facings* cherry  *Badges and Devices* — *On buttons* collar of tunic helmet forage cap and field cap —(Also worn by Indian officers in silver on the collar of full dress and on the pagri)—Two crossed dahs  *On pouch* — ' XCI " *On pouch belt* —Crossed unsheathed dahs and bugle ; ' 91 in upper angle ; joining handles of dahs a fancy scroll inscribed " Punjabis " ; the whole surrounded by a laurel wreath and surmounted by a Tudor crown

**92nd Punjabis** —*Uniform* drab ; *facings* white  *Badges and Devices* —*On pouch, forage cap and field cap* —In silver, the white elephant of Burma surrounded by a gilt Sikh quoit inscribed ' 92 Punjabis '  The whole surmounted by a Tudor crown  *On pouch belt* —In silver the white elephant of Burma ; below, ' Ava ' surrounded by a gilt laurel wreath surmounted by a Tudor crown  " 92 Punjabis  on a scroll below.

**93rd Burma Infantry** —*Uniform* drab ;  *facings* yellow  *Badges and Devices* — *On buttons.* — 93  *On collar of tunic forage cap and field cap* —A silver Royal Burmese peacock  *On pouch* — ' 93  in silver  *On pouch belt* —A laurel wreath surmounted by a Tudor crown  Within the wreath  the Royal Burmese peacock  Below the peacock a scroll inscribed '93rd Burma Infantry "

**94th Russell's Infantry** —*Uniform* scarlet ; *facings* dark green. *Badges and Devices.*— *On buttons* — 94  raised ; ' Russell's Infantry " raised on a scroll below  *On forage cap.*— A demi lion rampant with ' 94th Russell's Infantry " on a scroll below

**95th Russell's Infantry** —*Uniform* scarlet; *facings* dark green  *Badges and Devices.*— *On buttons* —A demi lion rampant ; below a scroll inscribed ' Russell's Infantry ' with 95 ' above it.  *On helmet and field cap* —In silver a demi lion rampant ; scroll with ' Russell's—95th—Infantry " below

**96th Berar Infantry** —*Uniform* scarlet ; *facings* dark green  *Badges and Devices.*— *On buttons* — 96.   *On helmet and field cap* —In silver ' 96  surmounted by a Tudor crown and  Berar' on scroll below

**97th Deccan Infantry** —*Uniform* scarlet ; *facings* dark green  *Badges and Devices.*— *On buttons* —' 97 ' surmounted by a Tudor crown and enclosed in a laurel wreath ; ' Deccan " inscribed on the edge above the crown and ' Infantry  on the edge below the wreath  *On helmet* (Indian officers—pagri).  A collar or band encircling ' 97 " and bearing a Maltese cross at each of its four points and four lozenges between each cross ; it is surmounted by a Tudor crown and encircled by a laurel wreath ; underneath a scroll inscribed Nagpore " ' Deccan Infantry '  *On forage cap and field cap* —Crossed colours surmounted by a Tudor crown, flanking an oval collar or band inscribed  Deccan Infantry ' with  97 " in centre and scroll below inscribed  Nagpore "

**98th Infantry** —*Uniform* scarlet ; *facings* dark green.  *Badges and Devices* —*On but tons* —' 98  within a laurel wreath surmounted by a Tudor crown.  *On helmet and forage cap.*—An eight pointed star, in the centre of which is a raised scroll, surmounted by a Tudor crown and  Infantry " on scroll  In centre of badge a raised " 98 "

**99th Deccan Infantry** —*Uniform* scarlet ; *facings* dark green  *Badges and Devices* — *On buttons* — 99  in centre and ' Deccan Infantry ' round the edge surmounted by a Tudor crown  *On helmet and forage cap* — 99 " in white metal silver plated, surmounted by a Tudor crown

**The 101st Grenadiers** —*Uniform* scarlet ; *facings* white  *Badges and Devices* —*On but tons.* — ' 101  beneath a grenade  *On collar of tunic* —(White metal horse for khaki and white clothing ) A gold embroidered grenade with the White Horse in silver on a brass ball *On forage cap* —Gold embroideied grenade with White Horse (silver) on ball

**102nd King Edward's Own Grenadiers** —*Uniform* scarlet ; *facings* white *Badges and Devices* —*On buttons.*—The Royal and Imperial Cypher of King Edward VII and Crown, surrounded by " 102nd Grenadiers " *On collar of tunic* (Indian officers, in gilt metal and silver)—gold embroidered grenade The Prince of Wales' plume and the Sphinx (with " Egypt ") in silver on the ball *On forage cap* — A gold embroidered grenade with the Sphinx (with " Egypt ") on the ball. *On pagri* (*Indian* ranks).—Grenade in biass with plume of the Prince of Wales in white metal on the flame, the Sphinx (with ' Egypt)" in white metal on the ball

**103rd Mahratta Light Infantry** —*Uniform* scarlet ; *facings* black *Badges and Devices* — *On buttons* —' 103 " between the strings of a bugle encircled by a wreath and surmounted by a Tudor crown *On collar of tunic.* —Silver horn with ' 103 ' in centre *On field cap* —Two small mounted buttons with 103 within a silver horn surmounted by a Tudor crown A brass badge, 103 " within a bugle surmounted by a Tudor crown

**104th Wellesley's Rifles** —*Uniform* dark green ; *facings* scarlet *Badges and Devices* — *On buttons.*—Bugle and Tudor crown with 104" in centre. *On pouch* —Silver bugle with " Wellesley's ' on scroll underneath *On pouch belt* —Solid Maltese cross on burnished plate encircled by laurel wreath and scroll surmounted by a Tudor crown Bugle in a circle in centre Honorary distinctions of the 104th 123rd and 125th Rifles on cross and scrolls of wreath. Silver whistle suspended by three chains each 14 inches long to a silver bugle surmounted by a Tudor crown

**105th Mahratta Light Infantry** —*Uniform* scarlet; *facings* black. *Badges and Devices.*— *On buttons* —A plain bugle surmounted by a Tudor crown The letter ' M " between the bugle strings *On collar of tunic* —Plain gilt bugle *On field cap* —Two small regimental buttons in front with a gilding metal bugle

**106th Hazara Pioneers** —*Uniform* drab ; *facings* ied *Badges and Devices.*— *On forage cap and field cap.*— 106 ' surmounted by a Tudor crown in silver on a drab braid boss *On pouch.*— 106 ' surrounded by a laurel wreath and surmounted by a Tudor crown " Hazara Pioneers on scroll below The whole in silver *On pouch belt* —A silver Maltese cross on a burnished silver plate surrounded by a laurel wreath and surmounted by a Tudor crown In the centre of the cross ' 106 " within a circle inscribed " Hazara Pioneers ; between each of the arms of the cross, a silver lion rampant

**107th Pioneers** —*Uniform* scarlet ; *facings* white *Badges and Devices* —*On buttons* — In gilt, raised crossed axes with a Tudor crown above *On collar of tunic and forage cap* —Gilt crossed axes *On helmet* —Silver gilt circular scroll containing in the centre crossed axes in silver Around the rim 107th Pioneers " in gilt *On waist plate* —In silver, crossed axes in centre. 107th Pioneers " on rim in silver gilt *On pouch and pouch belt* —As on helmet but surmounted by a Tudor crown

**108th Infantry** — *Uniform* scarlet ; *facings* white — *Badges and Devices* —*On buttons* — " 108 ' inside an arch round the upper edge of which is the word Infantry ' The whole enclosed in a laurel wreath and surmounted by a Tudor crown. *On forage cap* — 108 " embroidered in gold on the black band *On field cap* —As on forage cap but on a dark blue ground.

**109th Infantry.**— *Uniform* scarlet ; *facings* black —*Badges and Devices* —*On buttons* — " 109 ' surrounded by a collar inscribed Infantry ' surmounted by a Iudor ciown *On collar of tunic forage cap and field cap* —A silver Maltese cross with beaded points at the four corners In brass in the centre 109 surrounded by a collar inscribed Seringapatam " surmounted by a Tudor crown ; remainder of collar surrounded by laurel wieath

**110th Mahratta Light Infantry.**—*Uniform* scarlet ; *facings* black *Badges and Devices* —As for the 105th Mahratta Light Infantry

**112th Infantry** —*Uniform* scarlet ; *facings* yellow *Badges and Devices* —*On buttons* —" 112 " surmounted by a Tudor crown and surrounded by a laurel wreath *On forage cap and field cap* — 112 "

**113th Infantry** —*Uniform* scarlet ; *facings* yellow *Badges and Devices* —*On buttons* — ' 113 surmounted by a Iudor crown. *On collar of tunic* —The Sphinx (with " Egypt ') in brass *On field cap* —Sphinx in silver and gold embroidery.

**114th Mahrattas** —*Uniform* scarlet ; *facings* yellow *Badges and Devices* —*On buttons* —" 114 ' surmounted by a Tudor crown within a circle of raised laurel branches *On field cap.*—Polished silver star with Mahrattas ' in polished raised letters on a dull ground between two polished raised circles ; within the inner circle 114 " on a black or navy blue ground of cloth kept in position by a removable plate ; above a silver Iudor crown resting on outer circle

**116th Mahrattas** —*Uniform* scarlet ; *facings* yellow *Badges and Devices* — On buttons and field cap —As for the 114th Mahrattas but with the No 116

**117th Mahrattas** —*Uniform* scarlet ; *facings* yellow. *Badges and Devices* —*On buttons and field cap* —As for the 114th Mahrattas but with the No. ' 117.'

**119th Infantry (The Mooltan Regiment)** —*Uniform* scarlet ; *facings* yellow *Badges and Devices.*—*On buttons* — 119 ' surmounted by a Tudor crown encircled by laurel branches. *On Mess waistcoat* —plain gilt with ' 119 ' mounted *On forage cap and field cap* — 119 ' surmounted by a Tudor crown and crossed by two scrolls bearing the words " The Mooltan Regiment '

**120th Rajputana Infantry** —*Uniform* scarlet ; *facings* yellow   *Badges and Devices*   On *buttons* —" 120 " with circle round containing the words " Rajputana Infantry " Circle surmounted by a Tudor crown   *On Mess waistcoat*—plain gilt with " 120 " surmounted by a small Tudor crown, both mounted in silver.   *On forage cap and field cap* —The Lion and the Rising Sun ; the latter inscribed " Persia '   Below the lion " 120   and a scroll inscribed " Rajputana Infantry " beneath

**121st Pioneers** —*Uniform*  scarlet ; *facings*  white   *Badges and Devices* —On *buttons* —Crossed axes surmounted by a Tudor crown.   *On collar of tunic.*—Gilt crossed axes   *On helmet* —Silver crossed axes in a gilt ribbon scroll inscribed ' 121st Pioneers " The whole surmounted by a Tudor crown   *On forage cap* —Crossed axes worked in silver thread, surrounded by a laurel wreath worked in gold thread and surmounted by a similarly worked Tudor crown.

**122nd Rajputana Infantry** —*Uniform* scarlet ; *facings* emerald green.   *Badges and Devices* —On *buttons* —" 122  with scroll inscribed ' Rajputana " surrounded by a wreath of olive leaves   (The mess waistcoat and forage cap button is plain gilt, flat, with " 122 " in silver )   *On forage cap and field cap* —In silver '122 ' surmounted by a Tudor crown.

**123rd Outram's Rifles** —*Uniform* dark-green ; *facings* scarlet   *Badges and Devices* —On *buttons* - A bugle and Tudor crown with ' 123 " in the centre   *On forage cap.*—Silver bugle on a red braided boss   *On pouch* —As for the 104th Wellesley's Rifles but with " Outram s ' on the scroll   *On pouch belt.*—As for 104th Wellesley's Rifles

**124th Duchess of Connaught's Own Baluchistan Infantry** —*Uniform* drab (red serge trousers) ; *facings* scarlet   *Badges and Devices.*—On *buttons and waist plate*—" 124 " surmounted by a Tudor crown, with the words   Baluchistan Infantry '   *On forage cap and field cap.*—In silver two jezails crossed with ' 124 " in the lower angle   *On pouch* — " 124 " within a laurel wreath in gilt   *On pouch belt* —Brass plate bearing the honorary distinctions of the regiment.

**125th Napier's Rifles.**—*Uniform* dark green ; *facings* scarlet.   *Badges and Devices* —On *buttons.*—A bugle and Tudor crown with ' 125 ' in the centre   *On forage cap.*—As for 123rd Outram's Rifles   *On pouch* —As for the 104th Wellesley's Rifles, but with" Napier's" on the scroll   *On pouch belt* —As for 104th Wellesley's Rifles

**126th Baluchistan Infantry** —*Uniform* drab (red serge trousers) ; *facings* scarlet   *Badges and Devices* —On *buttons and waist plate* —  126 " surmounted by a Tudor crown sur rounded by a scroll inscribed ' Baluchistan Infantry '   *On forage cap and field cap* — Crossed Afghan knives with   126 " across the fortes   *On pouch*—" 126 " within a laurel wreath in gilt   *On pouch belt* —Brass plate bearing the honorary distinctions of the regiment

**127th Queen Mary's Own Baluch Light Infantry** —*Uniform* green (red serge trousers) ; *facings* scarlet   *Badges and Devices* —On *buttons* —Light Infantry bugle with Queen s crown above and ' 127th Baluch L. I   be'ow   *On shoulder* —Black metal Light In fantry bugle with " 127 Baluch " below   *On pouch* —Silver Light Infantry bugle   *On pouch belt* —Mi ltese cross encircled by a laurel wreath, in centre of cross a crescent in scribed " Baluch Light Infantry " and " 127 " above.   The battle honours of the regiment inscribed on the four outer sides of the cross— ' Delhi ', ' Abyssinia ", " Afghanistan  1879  1880 " ' Burma, 1885 1887 '', scroll  inscribed   British  East Africa, 1897 1899   below Maltese cross.   A scroll above the Maltese cross inscribed ' Queen Mary s Own ' and sur mounted by the Queen's crown

**128th Pioneers** —*Uniform* scarlet ; *facings* white   *Badges and Devices.*—On *but tons* —As for the 107th Pioneers   *On collar of tunic* —Gilt crossed axes   *On helmet and waist plate* —As for the 107th Pioneers but with " 128th Pioneers " round the rim   *On field cap* —Gilt crossed axes   *On the forage cap* —Silver crossed axes with " 128 " between the helves   *On pouch* —As on helmet but surmounted by a Tudor crown   *On pouch belt.*—As on pouch

**129th Duke of Connaught's Own Baluchis** —*Uniform* green (red serge trousers); *facings* scarlet   *Badges and Devices.* – On *forage cap and field  cap* —Silver bugle on a red boss. *On pouch* —Silver bugle  with knotted cords   *On pouch belt* —A Maltese cross surmounted by a Tudor crown encircled by a laurel wreath.   In the centre a crescent inscribed   129th Baluchis   and on the arms of the cross ' Persia ', ' Bushire ',   Kooshab ' ' Reshire ". The laurel wreath is inscribed   Duke of Connaught's Own".   A scroll above, inscribed ' Egypt, 1882 " " 'lel el Kebir ' and another below inscribed " Kandahar, 1880 " 'Afghanis tan  1878 80 '

**130th  King George's Own Baluchis (Jacob's Rifles)** —*Uniform* green (red serge trousers) ; *facings* scarlet   *Badges and Devices* —On *collar of tunic* —Prince of Wales's plumes in white metal   *On helmet* —Prince of Wales's plumes in silver with scroll underneath inscribed ' K G O Baluchis   *On forage and field cap* —Prince of Wales's plumes in silver   *On pouch* —The [Royal and Imperial Cypher surmounted by a Tudor crown, *On pouch belt* —A laurel wreath surmounted by the Prince of Wales s plumes " enclosing a Maltese cross, in the centre of which  is  a  crescent  with ' 130 " inside and " K G. O Baluchis   inscribed on the crescent, " China, 1900 " inscribed on top bar of Maltese cross, underneath, a scroll with ' Afghanistan, 1878-1880 '

**1st King George's Own Gurkha Rifles** (The Malaun Regiment).—*Uniform* dark green; *facings* scarlet    *Badges and Devices* —On buttons.—Crosssd khukris with ' 1 " in upper angle and a stringed bugle in the lower    On helmet —Crossed khukris with the plume of the Prince of Wales in the upper angle ; in the lower a stringed bugle surmounted by the figure ' 1 '    On forage and field cap.—The Prince of Wales's plume and coronet cross ed khukrls edge downwards with    1 " in upper angle    On red boss    On pouch —Silver bugle    On pouch belt —The Royal and Imperial Cypher surmounted by an Imperial crown above crossed khukries edge downwards ; a stringed bugle surmounted by " 1 " in the lower angle    The whole encircled by laurel leaves intwined by scrolls, bearing the honorary distinctions of the regiment ; below a scroll over the junction of the laurel branches in scribed " King George's Own Gurkha Rifles "

**2nd King Edward's Own Gurkha Rifles** (The Sirmoor Rifles).—*Uniform* dark green ; *facings* scarlet    *Badges and Devices.*—On buttons.—Crossed *khukris*, edge downwards surmounted by the Royal and Imperial Cypher of King Edward VII    On helmet, forage cap, field cap and pouch.—The Prince of Wales' plume in bronze (on a red boss    on the field cap).    On pouch belt —Within a laurel wreath, bronze, bearing the honorary distinc tions of the regiment silver, two crossed *khukris* (blades ilver, handles bronze) edge and handles downwards ; above the Royal and Imperial Cypher and Crown of King Edward VII In the lower    angle of the *khukris*    the letters " S E. R " intertwined ; below this the word " Delhi " below which again is a scroll inscribed ' King Edward's Own    All in silver, whistle and chain in bronze, attached to the belt by ram's head in bronze

**3rd Queen Alexandra s Own Gurkha Rifles** —*Uniform* dark green ; *facings* black    *Badges and Devices* —On buttons crossed *khukris*, edge upwards with ' 3 " in upper angle    On helmet, crossed *khukris* edge upwards with " 3    in upper angle ; surmounted with the Royal and Imperial Cypher ensigned with the Imperial Crown    On forage cap as oh helmet but smaller    On field cap as on helmet, but smaller ; a silver bugle on cap peak button    The same design as on the forage cap but surmounted with the Cypher of H. M    Queen    Alexandra with the Imperial Crown    worn by Gurkha Officers on the Kilmarnock cap    On pouch belt —A Maltese cross : in centre of cross two crossed *khukris*, edge upwards with    3 " in upper angle encircled by a band inscribed ' 3rd Gurkha Rifles    Above the cross    the word ' Delhi    Surmounted with the Royal and Imperial Cypher of Queen Alexandra ensigned with the Imperial Crown    Around the cross a laurel wreath intertwined with a scroll bearing the honorary distinctions of the regiment and the title ' Queen Alexandra's Own    On Pouch as on helmet.

**4th Gurkha Rifles** —*Uniform* dark green ; *facings* black    *Badges and Devices* —On buttons —    4 ' within a stringed bugle.    On helmet.—An eight pointed radiating bronze star in the centre of which is a silver eight pointed Maltese cross, surmounted by a silver Tudor crown    In centre of cross a silver bugle with strings inside which is    IV ' The Maltese cross surrounded by a bronze laurel wreath    Below, in silver crossed *khukris* edge downwards    On forage cap —A bugle    On pouch —Silver bugle with strings On pouch belt —A silver laurel wreath surmounted by a Tudor crown enclosing a Maltese cross in centre of which is a stringed bugle within a circle    A small silver lion between each of the arms of the cross

**5th Gurkha Rifles (Frontier Force)** —*Uniform* dark green ; *facings* black    *Badges and Devices* —On buttons helmet    waist plate (Gurkha officers only) *forage cap* (in silver) — Crossed khukris with ' 5 " in centre.    On pouch (Binocular case) —Crossed *khukris* and 5 " with scroll inscribed    Gurkhas " above.    On pouch belt —In silver a laurel wreath with scroll intertwined inscribed with the honorary distinctions of the regiment    The wreath surmounted by a Tudor crown    Within the wreath    an eight pointed star inside which is inscribed, within two plain circular lines    Gurkhas '    In the centre of the badge 5 " on a plain disc

**6th Gurkha Rifles** —*Uniform* dark green ; *facings* black    *Badges and Devices* —On buttons and helmet - Crossed *khukris* edge downwards and    6 ' between the handles    On collar of tunic and mess jacket —Crossed *khukris*, edge downwards.    On forage cap and pouch —As on buttons with a scroll below inscribed ' Gurkha Rifles "    On pouch belt —A Maltese cross within a laurel wreath surmounted by a Tudor crown    with a lion in each angle of the cross    Centre of cross a circular scroll with raised crossed *khukris*, edge downwards in centre with    6    between the handles    Scroll inscribed    Gurkha Rifles ' Below cross a scroll inscribed    Burma 1885 87 '    Whistle below centre ornament attached to lion s head above centre ornament by 3 chains 13½ inches long

**7th Gurkha Rifles** —*Uniform* dark green ; *facings* black    *Badges and Devices.*—On buttons and helmet —Crossed *khukris* edge upwards with    7 " in upper angle.    Forage cap field cap and pouch    In silver as on buttons    Pouch belt —In silver a Maltese cross charged with a scroll inscribed    Gurkha Rifles    encircling two *khukris* crossed edge upwards having    7 ' in the upper angle ; between the arms of the cross four lions ; the whole surmounted by a Tudor crown

**8th Gurkha Rifles** —*Uniform* dark green ; *facings* black    *Badges and Devices* —On buttons and helmet —Crossed khukris with    8 " in upper angle    On forage cap —In silver as on buttons    On pouch —In silver as on buttons but with a scroll below inscribed    Gurkha Rifles "    On pouch belt —A silver Maltese cross surrounded by a laurel wreath in the centre, two crossed *khukris*; '8 in upper angle the whole within a band inscribed "Gurkha Rifles." Above, a Tudor crown and Burma 1885 87.'

**9th Gurkha Rifles** —*Uniform* dark green; *facings* black. *Badges and Devices* —*On buttons, forage cap and field cap* —Crossed *khukris* edge downwards, with ' 9 ' in lower angle. *On helmet* (Gurkha officers Kilmarnock cap) —In silver, as on buttons *On pouch.*—Silver bugle with strings *On pouch belt* - Silver Maltese cross encircled by wreath; in centre '9 " within a band inscribed 'Gurkhas " Above a Tudor crown

**10th Gurkha Rifles** —*Uniform* dark green; *facings* black *Badges and Devices.* —*On buttons forage cap and pouch* —Bugle suspended by knotted strings *On helmet* (Gurkha officers—Kilmarnock cap) —Crossed *khukris* edge downwards and 10 ' in upper angle *On pouch belt* —Bugle suspended by knotted strings, crossed by *khukri*, edge downwards with " X ' thereon Scroll underneath inscribed "Gurkha Rifles." The whole enclosed within a laurel wreath surmounted by a Tudor crown and straight bar immediately below

## APPENDIX No. II

### BELT AND SWORD KNOT (UNIVERSAL PATTERN).

### (a) The " Sam Browne " Belt

( Worn by officers of all branches of the service )

The belts complete consist of a waist belt, two shoulder belts, a sword frog, an ammunition pouch and a pistol case ; the whole made of brown (or black) bridle leather.

The waist belt is 2½ inches wide and of a length to suit the wearer It is fitted with a double tongued brass buckle, and has four brass dees for the shoulder belts (two at the back and one at each side), a running loop for the free end of the belt, two brass rings for attachment of the frog, and a hook for hooking it up The waist belt is lined with faced basil

The shoulder belts are plain straps (crossed at the back through a loop) They are 1½ inches wide The patterns are about 35 inches long over all, without chapes The length, however may be varied to suit the wearer They are fitted with studs for attachment to the dees at the back of the waist belt A chape, with stud and a buckle is provided for each for attachment to the dees at the sides of the belt

The strap over the left shoulder need not be worn except when the revolver is carried

The frog is fitted with two straps which are to be passed through the dees on the lower part of the belt. The frog has a small brass dee on the top to go over the hook on the belt when ' hooking up " A stud is fitted on the front of the frog, upon which the tab of the scabbard supporter is fastened. (*See* description of leather scabbard )

A small strap for steadying the sword hilt is attached to the rear dee for the frog, holes being made in the strap to pass over a stud on the belt above the front dee

The ammunition pouch and pistol-case are fitted with loops on the back for attachment to the waist belt ; also with stud and tab fastenings The loop on the pistol case is furnished with a small brass hook, which should pass through a hole to be made for the purpose in the belt to suit the wearer, in order to secure the case and keep it in position

The pattern pistol case is to be regarded as typical only, as its dimensions must suit the particular pattern of pistol carried

The " furniture " should be of the best yellow brass

### (b) Web Sword Belt

This consists of a waist belt and a shoulder suspender of worsted web, strengthened at various parts with black morocco leather It is furnished with gilding chapes and dees The loops and chapes are of morocco leather and the furniture of gilding metal.

The suspender is fitted with hooks so that it can be removed by officers wearing the web belt under the sash, outside the frock coat

### (c) Sword knot

The sword knot to be used with the Sam Browne, belt is the universal pattern of brown (or black) leather It is a plain strap made of pig skin best bridle leather or calf, the ends being secured into an acorn ' having plaited leather covering It is furnished with a sliding keeper

Length of strap in the double 15 inches ; width of strap, ⅝ inch ; length of acorn, 2½ inches

### (d) Web Belt and Bridle Leather straps for carrying Great coat

The belt is made from 2½ inch worsted web and is strengthened at the eyelet holes by a light piece of leather The coat straps are made from buff leather, and the furniture of gilding metal

## APPENDIX No III

### BUTTONS AND LACE

**Buttons**—Buttons are of the following sizes :—

|  |  |
|---|---|
| Large | 35 to 40 lines (Hussars 32 lines). |
| Medium | 30 to 34   , |
| Small | 24 to 29   , |
| Gorget | 20 lines |

**Lace, Quality of**—The standard quality recommended for gold lace is as follows :—

|  |  |  |
|---|---|---|
| Gold | 3 500 | } per cent |
| Silver | 87 334 | |
| Alloy | 9 166 | |

The lace should be mercurial gilt

For laces more than ½ inch wide  the thread should be 4 drachm, and wire  ' 20 fine '

For narrower laces, the thread should be 3½ drachm  and wire ' 20 extra fine "

---

## APPENDIX No IV

### CARE AND PRESERVATION OF UNIFORM

#### (a) Care and preservation of uniform and of gold lace

Articles of uniform liable to be moth eaten  should be unfolded at intervals and well beaten and brushed in the open air   Russia leather parings powdered camphor naphthaline carbolised paper or turpentine sprinkled on brown paper  or on the garments, are good for the prevention of moth, and one or other of these preventives should be placed amongst articles of uniform which are to be packed away for any time

Before being packed away gold lace  braid cord, or buttons on garments should be covered with tissue paper  and then placed in tin lined air tight cases.   Care must be taken to use paper that is thoroughly dry   For the prevention of moth  the garments should be  well aired and brushed before being packed

Gold  trimmings  and gold  lace that have become slightly tarnished can be cleaned with a mixture of cream of tartar and dry bread rubbed up very fine applied in a  dry  state  and brushed lightly with a clean soft brush

#### (b) Removing stains from scarlet tunics or frocks

In  many cases stains may be removed by the part affected being rubbed with dry pipeclay and then well brushed with a clean brush   Should this fail to remove  them  the  following mixture may be tried:—

⅓ ounce of salts of sorrel to ⅓ a pint of boiling water

⅓ ounce of cream of tartar to ⅓ a pint of cold water

Each solution should be kept in a separate flat vessel

These quantities will be sufficient to clean 2 or 3 garments

The garment which requires cleaning  should be first well beaten and brushed, and a perfectly clean hard brush should be used in applying the solutions

The solutions should be applied alternately commencing with the salts of sorrel, until the garment has been washed all over, and all the stains removed

If the weather permit the cleaned garments should be hung up in the sun to dry ; if not, they should be hung up in a dry place  but not near fires or stoves

---

## APPENDIX No V

### REVOLVER

### Description of the latest pattern of Service " Pistol, Webley, Mark IV "

This pistol belongs to the class of extracting revolvers   The calibre is 441 inch   The principal parts are the barrel,  the cylinder  and the body

The barrel is jointed to the body and held in position for firing by the rib extending back on to the body and is firmly secured by the barrel catch

The cylinder is chambered to hold 6 cartridges, and is mounted to the barrel on a fixed axis, and held in position at the time of extracting by the cam

The stem of the extractor lies in the fixed  axis  surrounded  by  a  spiral  spring which returns the extractor after ejecting the cartridge cases ; the extractor is forced out by  a  small lever in the joint as the barrel is being rotated on the joint pin

When it is necessary to remove the cylinder for cleaning  the fixing screw must be unscrewed, and the pistol opened to its fullest extent ;  then  by  pressing the lever against the cam the cylinder will be free ;  in no other position can the cylinder be taken off the axis.

The body is fitted with a shield plate of hardened steel to prevent wear of firing hole, and to support base of cartridge

Weight of pistol about 2 lbs 3 oz

Cartridge charge, about 7½ grains of cordite     Bullet, about 265 grains

## APPENDIX No VI

### SADDLERY

## Description of Universal Pattern

*Collar, head.*—Of bridle leather.  The head, nose band and back stay are 1¼ inches in width  and the throat lash ¾ inch in width    The collar is fitted with brass buckles, squares and rings, and is without rosettes.

*Bit Portmouth reversible*—Is of steel with medium port  and is without bosses  rein rings, and lower bar.  It has rein loops and slots in the cheeks.

*Head bridle*—Of bridle leather and detachable   It is ¾ inch wide  and fitted with brass buckles

*Reins bit*—Of bridle leather, ⅞ inch wide, and fitted with brass buckles

*Bit, bridoon*—Of wrought iron  with plain mouthpiece 6 inches in width, rings 1¾ inches in diameter and with tees 5¼ inches in length

*Reins bridoon*—Of bridle leather, ¾ inch in width, sewn on to the bridoon

*Cases horse shoe, near and off*—Bridle leather 5¾ inches deep by 6½ inches wide  the insides are fitted with  nail pockets   Each has two suspending straps ¾ inch in width fitted with brass buckles

The near case is fitted with a leather tube for carrying the sword scabbard, and a steady ing strap.

*Girths.*—Of dark blue woollen web  one 5 inches and the other 2⅞ inches  each fitted with solid nickel buckles.

*Rope, head*—Of white cotton 1¼ inches, 3 strand rope, fitted at one end with a brown leather billet and a 1 inch brass buckle, and the other end whipped

*Saddle*—Seat of hogskin  set with white wool flock and serge, and with a seam in cantle, length of seat about 17¾ inches

Flaps, solid, skirt leather  hogskin printed being 18¼ inches in length, by 12¼ inches in width  and are without rolls

The side bars project in front and extend in rear, total length about 23½ inches

The pannels are of leather back and front stuffed with best white wool flock

*Leathers stirrup*—Of stirrup butt 1⅜ inches in width and fitted with 1⅜ inches solid nickel buckles

*Stirrups*—Of solid nickel or steel  hollow tread 4⅓ inches by 2¼ inches  height 4¼ in hes

*Surcingle*—Of bridle leather  body 2¼ inches wide

*Straps.*—Of bridle leather

|  |  |  |
|---|---|---|
| Cloak  centre  . | 26½ inches | × ¾ inch |
| Cloak and Wallet | 46 | × ¾ |
| Baggage | 34 | × ⅜ |

*Wallets.*—The backs are of crop leather, the connecting band of bridle leather  the other parts of bag hide   They are waterproof lined    The inside of near wallet is fitted with an ammunition pocket, and the off one with a loop for pistol

NOTE—In addition to the foregoing articles officers may provide themselves with a saddle bag or with a despatch bag, patterns of which can be seen at the War Office   The specification of the latter can be obtained from Army Headquarters India

## APPENDIX No VII

## Shoulder Chains

The rings must be made of the best hard drawn steel  wire, which when faced together will make a diameter of  065 inch   The external diameter of the rings to be  4 inch   The chains are to contain 319 links  and weigh from 4 to 4½ ozs ; they must be  perfectly sound  well finished  and in all respects equal to the sealed pattern,  The chain must resist a tensile strain of not less than 160 lbs.  and the permanent elongation after such strain must not exceed $\frac{1}{16}$ inch over the full length of the shoulder chain,  The breaking strain must be not less than 224 lbs, applied over the uniform width of  11 links  with attachments to 5 links so that weight is applied from end to end of the shoulder chain

## APPENDIX No VIII

### SWORDS AND SCABBARDS

## British Officers Of Indian Cavalry

*Sword.*—The blade is slightly curved, tapers gradually, is 35 inches long from  shoulder to point, and is fullered on both sides commencing 1½ inches from hilt, to about 9 inches from point to a thickness of not less than 0·4 inch.

The mounting consists of guard grip, ferrule strap, nut and washer

The guard grip, and ferrule are held in position by a nut screwed on the tang under neath the strap ; the strap is held by a washer  the end of the tang being riveted over the washer

The guard is of stamped mild steel, of the bar pattern

The grip is of wood covered with fish skin and bound with silver wire ; the length of grip must be from 5 inches to 5¾ inches long, variation being allowed to suit the size of the hand.

The blade may be plain  or ornamentally embossed   In the latter case, while it is not necessary that a uniform pattern of ornamentation should be followed  the design should not include any badge or device beyond the Royal Cypher and Crown, and  the  usual manufacturer's name or trade mark

Swords of this pattern should stand the following tests :—

*Blade* —In set and stiffened stage :—Struck back and edge, and on both flats, on an oak block by hand

With a weight of 26 lbs. in the vertical testing machine, the blade should recover straightness after not less than 1 inch depression ; in the same machine it should be shortened 4½ inches by bending from right to left and then from left to right.

*Hilt assembled* —Struck a moderate blow on an oak block, back and edge  to test the soundness of hilting

*Sword complete* —With a weight of 24 lbs  in the vertical testing machine it should recover straightness after not less than 1 inch depression.

*Scabbard* —The scabbard is of steel ; it is fitted with a German silver mouthpiece with the sputcheon brazed on, fixed to the scabbard with two screws ; two bands with loose rings are brazed  to the scabbard  2¼ inches and 10½ inches  respectively from the top of the mouthpiece

The lining is of leather, blocked flesh side out turned, butted  and herring bone stitched with fine waxed thread on the right side of lining, and held in position by the sputcheon

| | | |
|---|---|---|
| Length of Sword | | 3 feet  5¼  inches |
| , Scabbard | . | 2 , 11⅞ |
| , Blade from shoulder to point | | 2 , 11 |
| , Sword and scabbard | | 3 , 6⅛ , |
| Balance from hilt  about | | 5¼ |
| Weight of Sword | | 2 lbs |
| , Scabbard | | 15 ¼ ounces |
| ,, , , Lining | | 1⅓ |

## British Officers of Indian Infantry (except when otherwise stated) ; Supply and Transport Corps, and Indian Medical Service

*Sword* —The blade is straight, tapers gradually  is 32 9/16 inches long from  shoulder to point, and is fullered  on both sides  to a thickness of not less than 0·5 inch

The mountings consist of guard grip strap ferrule nut  and washer

The guard, grip  and ferrule  are held in position by a nut screwed on the tang ; the strap is held  by a ferrule and washer  the end of the tang  being  riveted  over  the washer

The guard is of  steel  and is pierced with an ornamental device the size of  the  perfora tion is important  so arranged as not to permit of a sword point passing through  so as to injure the hand

The grip is of wood  covered with fishskin  and bound  with silver wire : the  length of the grip  must be from 5 inches to 5¾ inches long  variation being allowed to suit the size of the hand.

The blade may be plain  or ornamentally embossed ; in the  latter case, while it is not necessary that a uniform pattern  of  ornamentation should be followed  the design should not include any badge or device beyond the Royal Monogram and Crown, and the  usual manufacturer's name or trade mark

Swords of this pattern should stand the following tests : —

*Blade.*—In set and stiffened stage :—Struck on back  and edge and on both flats  on an oak block by hand

With a  weight  of 34 lbs  in the vertical testing machine  the blade should recover straightness after not less than 1 inch depression ; in the same machine  the blade should be shortened 4 inches, by bending from right to left, and then from left to right.

*Hilt assembled* —Struck a moderate blow  on  an oak block  back  and edge, to test  the soundness of hilting

*Sword complete* —With a weight of 32 lbs  in the vertical testing machine  it should recover straightness after not less than 1 inch depression

*Scabbard* —The scabbard is of steel  it is fitted  with a German silver mouthpiece with  the  sputcheon  brazed on  fixed to the scabbard by two  screws ; two bands with loose rings are brazed on to the scabbard, $2\frac{1}{4}$ inches and $10\frac{3}{8}$ inches, respectively, from the top of the mouthpiece

The lining is of leather, blocked flesh side out, turned butted, and herring bone stitched with fine waxed thread on the right side of lining, and held in position by the sputcheon.

| | | | |
|---|---|---|---|
| Length of Sword | | 3 feet | $2\frac{1}{4}$ inches |
| , „ Scabbard | . . | 2 | $9\frac{3}{4}$ , |
| „ , Blade from shoulder to point | | 2 | $8\frac{1}{4}$ , |
| „ „ Sword and Scabbard | | 3 | $3\frac{3}{4}$ , |
| Balance from hilt about | | | $4\frac{1}{4}$ |
| Weight of Sword | | 2 lbs | |
| „ , Scabbard | | $15\frac{1}{4}$ ozs | |
| „ , Lining | | $1\frac{1}{4}$ „ | |

## Officers, Rifle Regiments.

*Sword.*—The blade is straight tapers gradually is $32\frac{9}{16}$ inches long from shoulder to point and is fullered $c_a$ both sides commencing 2 inches from the shoulder to about 17 inches from the point to a thickness of 035 inch

The mountings consist of guard grip, ferrule, nut strap and washer.

The guard grip and ferrule are held in position by a nut screwed on the tang, underneath the strap ; the strap is held by a washer the end of the tang being riveted over the washer

The guard is of malleable iron, or mild homogeneous steel nickel plated, ornamented with Royal Crown over the regimental device

The grip is of wood covered with fish skin and bound with silver wire ; the length of grip must be from 5 inches to $5\frac{3}{4}$ inches long, variation being allowed to suit the size of the hand.

The blade may be plain or ornamentally embossed in the latter case while it is not necessary that a uniform pattern of ornamentation should be followed, the design should not include any badge or device, beyond the Royal Cypher and Crown, and the usual manufacturer's name or trade mark.

Swords of this pattern should stand the following tests :—

*Blade.*—In set and stiffened stage :—Struck back and edge and on both flats on an oak block, by hand

With a weight of 17 lbs in the vertical testing machine the blade should recover straightness after not less than 1 inch depression ; in the same machine the blade should be shortened 4 inches, by bending from right to left and then from left to right

*Hilt assembled* —Struck a moderate blow on an oak block, to test the soundness of the hilting

*Sword complete* —With a weight of 15 lbs in the vertical testing machine, it should recover straightness after not less than 1 inch depression

*Scabbard.*—The scabbard is of steel (nickel plated) ; it is fitted with a German silver mouthpiece with the sputcheon brazed on, fixed to the scabbard with two screws ; two bands with loose rings are brazed on to the scabbard $2\frac{1}{16}$ inches and $10\frac{3}{8}$ inches respectively, from the top of the mouthpiece

The lining is of leather blocked flesh side out turned butted and herring bone stitched with waxed thread on the right side of the lining and held in position by the sputcheon

| | | | |
|---|---|---|---|
| Length of Sword | | 3 feet | $2\frac{1}{4}$ inches |
| , , Scabbard | . | 2 | $9\frac{1}{4}$ , |
| Blade from shoulder t ) point | | 2 | $8\frac{9}{16}$ , |
| „ „ Sword and Scabbard | | 3 | $3\frac{3}{4}$ , |
| Balance from hilt | | | $4\frac{1}{4}$ |
| Weight of Sword . | | 1 lb | $14\frac{1}{4}$ ounces |
| , Scabbard | | 1 lb | 4 , |
| „ „ „ Lining | | $1\frac{1}{4}$ „ | |

## Indian Officers, Infantry

*Sword* —The blade is straight, tapering gradually $32\frac{9}{16}$ inches long from shoulder to point and is fullered on both sides at the guard end

The mountings consist of guard, grip strap ferrule nut and washer with a buff leather washer placed on the blade under the guard

The guard grip and ferrule are held in position by a ferrule and washer, the tang being riveted over the washer

The guard is of steel and is pierced with an ornamental device with the Royal and Imperial Cypher on the outer boss of the hilt. The grip is $5\frac{1}{4}$ inches long.

The following tests are applied to swords before issue :—

*Blade* —In set and stiffened stage

Struck back and edge, on an oak block by hand and on both flats on a flat oak block by hand also

With a weight of 32 lbs in the vertical testing machine the blade is to recover straightness after not less than one inch depression

In the same machine the blade will be shortened 5 inches bending from left to right and then from right to left

*Blade.*—In polished stage

With a weight of 30 lbs. in the vertical testing machine, the blade is to recover straightness after not less than one inch depression   In the same machine, the blade will be shortened 5 inches bending from left to right only

*Hilt assembled* —Struck a moderate blow on an oak block back and edge, to test the soundness of hilting

*Sword complete.*—With a weight of 30lbs in the vertical testing machine, the sword is to recover straightness after not less than one inch depression

*Scabbard.*—The scabbard is of steel, fitted with a sputcheon brazed to the mouthpiece and fixed to the scabbard by 2 screws   Two bands with loose rings are brazed on the scabbard 2½ inches and 10¾ inches respectively from the top of the mouthpiece   The scabbard lining consists of two strips of wood held in position under the sputcheon

|  |  |  |
|---|---|---|
| Length of | ⎧ Sword | 3 feet 2¼⅜ inches |
|  | ⎪ Scabbard | 2 „ 10 „ |
|  | ⎨ Blade from point to shoulder | 2 „ 8⁹⁄₁₆ „ |
|  | ⎪ Sword and scabbard (with ½ inch buff | |
|  | ⎩   leather washer) | 3 „ 4¾ „ |
| Balance from hilt | 4½ to 5 inches | |

| | | |
|---|---|---|
| Weight of | ⎧ Sword | 2 lbs 1½ ozs |
|  | ⎨ | |
|  | ⎩ Scabbard | 14 , |

The swords will be issued with the edges ground to a thickness of 01 inch   the grinding of the front edge commencing at 15 inches from the point, and that of the back edge at 3 inches from the point

The majority of the swords will fit the scabbards ; in cases where they do not fit, the linings should be slightly reduced locally

## Scabbard for use with " Sam Browne " Belt

The scabbard is built up with two strips of wood grooved to receive blade of sword ; they are butted and glued together

The strips of wood are covered with brown (or black) leather sewn down one side   A raised rib is formed below the locket by a piece of packing between wood and leather

The body is made entirely of brown leather   including the chape   The supporter is attached to the rib of the scabbard to hold it at a proper height in the frog and has a tab attached which buttons on the front of belt frog or the frog on shoe pocket and so prevents either upward or downward movement of the scabbard

|  |  |
|---|---|
| Length over all | 2 feet 10 inches. |
| „   of chape | 7½ inches |
| Weight of scabbard complete | 9½ ounces |

The pattern scabbard is to be regarded as typical only, as shape and dimensions may require to be varied according to the sword to be carried

––––––––––

# APPENDIX No IX
## WATER BOTTLE
### Description of the Pattern with which officers are recommended to provide themselves

The bottle is made of pure aluminium shaped to fit the side of the wearer.  It is 5 25 inches deep, 7 25 inches wide, and 3 inches broad across top   The neck is 1 125 inch long

It has a cork stopper attached by a short chain   The cork is held on a stem, tapped at the end to receive a small nut so that the cork which is of the size generally used for wine bottles, etc , may be readily renewed when necessary.

The bottle is covered with felt, and has a strap fixed around it passing through four loops sewn on to the felt   The extremities of this strap which are at the shoulders of the bottle are provided with brass loops through which the ends of the sling or carrier are passed   The sling is ⅝ inch wide and of suitable length for the wearer   It has a brass stud fixed near each end and a hole at the end to button on to the stud   The sling may therefore be worn under belts, so as to carry the bottle steadily, and the latter may be removed without disturbing the sling   The leather is all brown ' best bridle "

Weight complete   about 14 ozs

Capacity of bottle, 2¼ pints

# APPENDIX No X

## WARRANT OFFICERS

As for Departmental Commissioned Officers with Honorary Rank, with the following exceptions :—

**Badges of Rank.**—The rank of warrant officers is shown by badges as under :—

### British

*Conductor* —Crown with laurel wreath

*Sub Conductor* —Crown

### Indian

*Sub Assistant Surgeon (1st Class)* —3 Stars

*Sub Assistant Surgeon (2nd Class)* —2 Stars

*Sub Assistant Surgeon (3rd Class)* —1 Star

The badges of warrant officers will be worn on the right forearm and will be of gold embroidery on the patrol and mess jackets and of gilding metal on other garments

**Gloves** —Brown leather in all orders of dress

**Mess Dress** —Optional

**Patrol Jacket** (*instead of Tunic and Serge Frock*) —*Ordnance Department* —Blue cloth, cut patrol shape body lined with black Italian cloth and the sleeves with striped Silesia   The jacket is made 26 inches long for a man 5 feet 7 8 inches   Scarlet cloth collar 2 inches deep lined with black Italian cloth, the corners being slightly rounded and fastened with 2 black hooks and eyes collar tab of buckram covered with black Italian cloth, black mohair braid tracing all round the collar ; for conductors a gold shoulder knot for sub conductors a gold twisted shoulder cord   Sleeves, no cuffs, but an Austrian knot of black mohair braid tracing the top of the knot being 8½ inches from the bottom of the sleeve and 2 inches at the fore and hind seams   An outside breast pocket, with a 1 inch box pleat down the centre and a three pointed flap on each breast the top of the flap being in line with the second button from the top   the depth of the pocket from the top of the flap is 7½ inches and the width 6¼ inches.   Openings at the bottom of the side seams 7½ inches at the left and 6 inches at the right   the side body being on top   Buttons—5 down the front, 2 on the shoulders and 2 on the pockets

*Army Clothing Department* —As for Ordnance  but with light blue cloth collar

*Army Remount Department* —As for Ordnance, but with yellow cloth collar

*Indian Subordinate Medical Department* —As for Ordnance  but with black silk velvet collar

*Military Farms Department* —As for Ordnance but with grass green cloth collar

*Military Prisons and Detention Barracks* —As for Ordnance  but with black cloth collar

*Miscellaneous List and Military Accounts, Military Works Services (including Barrack Public Works, Telegraphs Sappers and Miners) and Garrison and Depôt Staff* —As for Ordnance but with blue cloth collar

*Supply and Transport Corps* —As for Ordnance, but with white cloth collar

**Pouch Belt and Pouch** —Not worn

**Shoulder Strap Titles** —The following distinctive letters are worn on the shoulder straps of khaki jackets and great coats :—

| | |
|---|---|
| Army Remount Department | A R |
| Garrison Depôt and Musketry Staff  Chief Instructors of Central Gymnasia | G R I |
| Indian Subordinate Medical Department | I S M D. |
| Military Farms Department | Farms |
| Military Prisons and Detention Barracks | M P |
| Military Works Services (including Barrack) | M W |
| Miscellaneous Departments  except as provided elsewhere | Staff |
| Ordnance Department | O |
| Public Works Department  Conductors of Sappers and Miners | R E |
| Supply and Transport Corps | S T C |

**Sword Belt and Sword Knot**—Web belt with brown leather sling and knot   On active service and manœuvres, etc , the Sam Browne belt will be worn

### *Supply and Transport Corps*

As above with the following modifications :—

Pantaloons cord khaki ; gaiters mounted artillery ; great coat drab, mounted ; spurs hunting and swan neck ; helmet, complete with white covers ; putties and haversack

### *Sub Assistant Surgeons*

As described for Senior Sub Assistant Surgeons in para  220  with the following exceptions :—

**Patrol Jacket** (*instead of Tunic*) —Dark blue cloth, fastened with hooks and eyes down the front  and edged with inch black mohair braid all round including the collar and up the openings of the sides.   Shoulder straps of blue cloth edged with $\frac{1}{2}$ inch black mohair braid except at the base   Pockets in front edged with inch mohair braid,  pocket  inside left breast An Austrian knot of black cord, 9 inches high on the cuffs

### *General*

Uniform of the old pattern may be worn until unserviceable

The wearing of uniform by warrant officers of departments proceeding  home  on trans ports, on leave pending retirement, is optional

# INDEX

CALCUTTA : PRINTED BY SUPDT. GOVT PRINTING, INDIA, 8, HASTINGS STREET

www.ingramcontent.com/pod-product-compliance
Lightning Source LLC
Chambersburg PA
CBHW030400100426
42812CB00028B/2786/J